OUR UNIONS

A MANUAL OF METHODS
FOR
LOCAL, COUNTY, DISTRICT, AND
STATE CHRISTIAN ENDEAVOR
UNIONS

BY

AMOS R. WELLS

MANAGING EDITOR OF THE GOLDEN RULE,
AND AUTHOR OF "SOCIAL EVENINGS," "THE
JUNIOR MANUAL," "WAYS OF WORKING
SERIES," "FOREMAN JENNIE," ETC.

First Fruits Press
Wilmore, Kentucky
c2015

Our unions: a manual of methods for local, county, district, and state Christian Endeavor Unions, by Amos R. Wells.

First Fruits Press, ©2015
Previously published: Boston and Chicago: United Society of Christian Endeavor, ©1896.

ISBN: 9781621713821 (print), 9781621713838 (digital)

Digital version at http://place.asburyseminary.edu/christianendeavorbooks/20/

First Fruits Press is a digital imprint of the Asbury Theological Seminary, B.L. Fisher Library. Asbury Theological Seminary is the legal owner of the material previously published by the Pentecostal Publishing Co. and reserves the right to release new editions of this material as well as new material produced by Asbury Theological Seminary. Its publications are available for noncommercial and educational uses, such as research, teaching and private study. First Fruits Press has licensed the digital version of this work under the Creative Commons Attribution Noncommercial 3.0 United States License. To view a copy of this license, visit http://creativecommons.org/licenses/by-nc/3.0/us/.

For all other uses, contact:

First Fruits Press
B.L. Fisher Library
Asbury Theological Seminary
204 N. Lexington Ave.
Wilmore, KY 40390
http://place.asburyseminary.edu/firstfruits

Wells, Amos R. (Amos Russel), 1862-1933.
    Our unions : a manual of methods for local, county, district, and state Christian
    Endeavor Unions / by Amos R. Wells.
    122 pages ; 21 cm.
    Wilmore, Ky. : First Fruits Press, ©2015.
    Reprint. Previously published: Boston : United Society of Christian Endeavor, ©1896.
    ISBN: 9781621713821 (pbk.)
    1. International Society of Christian Endeavor. I. Title.
BV1426 .W5 2015

Cover design by Jonathan Ramsay

asburyseminary.edu
800.2ASBURY
204 North Lexington Avenue
Wilmore, Kentucky 40390

First Fruits
THE ACADEMIC OPEN PRESS OF ASBURY SEMINARY

First Fruits Press
The Academic Open Press of Asbury Theological Seminary
204 N. Lexington Ave., Wilmore, KY 40390
859-858-2236
first.fruits@asburyseminary.edu
asbury.to/firstfruits

OUR UNIONS

A Manual of Methods

FOR

LOCAL, COUNTY, DISTRICT, AND STATE
CHRISTIAN ENDEAVOR UNIONS

BY

AMOS R. WELLS

MANAGING EDITOR OF THE GOLDEN RULE, AND AUTHOR OF
"SOCIAL EVENINGS," "THE JUNIOR MANUAL,"
"WAYS OF WORKING SERIES,"
"FOREMAN JENNIE,"
ETC.

BOSTON AND CHICAGO
UNITED SOCIETY OF CHRISTIAN ENDEAVOR

C. J. PETERS & CO., TYPOGRAPHERS,
BOSTON.

1

CONTENTS.

3

OUR UNIONS.

CHAPTER I.

ORGANIZING A UNION.

The Value of Christian Endeavor Unions. — The useful purposes to which the church of Christ can put Christian Endeavor unions, and the useful results that spring from their work, may better be judged from the perusal of this book than from any preliminary statement. It may, however, be said in brief, first, that it is in the work of the city, county and State unions that Christian Endeavor interdenominational fellowship is especially shown. This fellowship is of course conspicuously manifested in the great International Conventions, but those crowded conventions, though their attendance number fifty thousand, reach few indeed of the vast Christian Endeavor host, while the work of the local union concerns all of the millions of young people banded together " for Christ and the church."

It is in the Christian Endeavor unions that the chief power of Christian Endeavor combination and co-operation is manifested. The unions are the organizations through which chiefly the best Christian Endeavor methods and the most advanced ideas of the organization can be spread. In the great gatherings of the State unions as well as in the crowded rallies of the local unions, the enthusiasm of large numbers is brought to the smallest .nd most struggling society.

Through the machinery of the local union the strength of the better equipped societies is communicated to the weaker ones, with no loss to the former. These unions are provocative of emulation to noble deeds. By wise use of them, the Christian ministers and the strong laymen of every community are enabled to influence far more than they otherwise would. As shown in many sections of this book, the practical working of State and local unions binds together the young people of any denomination for denominational purposes. These unions are training schools in co-operation and practical organization, and give the young people an education along these important lines that will prove invaluable to the church of a decade hence.

The social uses of these Christian Endeavor unions are manifold. Further, they unify the religious forces of a city for moral ends, since in not a few communities they afford the only working platform that draws together all the Protestant elements of a town or district.

All of these gains are to be obtained, of course, only in proportion as the union is carried on wisely and in accordance with the results of the best experience. To give this, so far as my observation and acquaintance with many unions and union workers will permit me, is the purpose of this book.

Organizing a Union. — In localities where no local union exists and where the societies are too few, or think they are too few, to form a union, a good step toward it is an informal meeting called for the purpose of discussing Christian Endeavor means and methods. Such meetings may be made profitable even if no more than two societies exist in a community, and they will soon grow into local unions. Indeed, it is my belief that a regularly organized local union of no more than two societies can do admirable work, so admirable that the union will soon come to consist of more societies.

The First Conferences. — The steps to be taken in the organization of a Christian Endeavor union are very simple. Let those interested in the movement consult the pastors at the outset and obtain their co-operation, consulting also the leaders of the societies and getting an informal expression of opinion.

If this is, on the whole, favorable, appoint a time and place where the pastors and the presidents of the societies that would be expected to join the proposed union may meet, and form a plan for the initial gathering. To this gathering should be invited all the societies. The first thing after a temporary organization, the appointment of president and secretary, should come a brief address explaining the advantages to be gained from a Christian Endeavor union. Following this the matter should be put to vote, whether the societies there present desire to form a Christian Endeavor union. Brief remarks upon this topic may be made by the pastors and prominent Endeavorers, and as soon as an affirmative vote has been taken, a committee on constitution should be appointed.

The Constitution. — This committee should have before it a constitution already prepared by representatives from the societies. The constitution of a union at its starting out should be exceedingly simple, and it will not take long for the committee to agree upon its fundamental articles. A caution is in place against the adoption of too much machinery at the start. Let it all come as a natural growth, and then it will be effective. While the committee is deliberating, the mass meeting should be listening to addresses on important Christian Endeavor matters.

At the close of the meeting the committee on constitution will make its report, the election of officers should be held, and a time and place fixed, if possible, for the next mass meeting, or the union may leave that to be determined by the executive committee.

CHAPTER II.

THE CONSTITUTION.

I GIVE below the forms of constitution recommended for State and local unions. It will be understood, of course, that these are mere outlines, to be filled out and modified as local needs may require.

CONSTITUTION FOR STATE UNIONS.

ARTICLE I. — *Name.*

The name of this Union shall be THE .... CHRISTIAN ENDEAVOR UNION.

ARTICLE II. — *Object.*

The object of the union shall be to stimulate an interest in Young People's Societies of Christian Endeavor and in local unions of the same in this State, and to promote their efficiency as factors in Christian life and church work by bringing them into closer relationship with one another through conferences, reports, and correspondence.

ARTICLE III. — *Members.*

Any society of Christian Endeavor, connected with an evangelical church in this State, whose constitution, in its aims and in its prayer-meeting obligations, conforms substantially in spirit to what is known as " The Model Constitution," may join in this union on its own vote to do so, communicated in writing to the secretary of this union, and approved by its executive committee. The members of any society belonging to this union will be entitled to all its privileges.

ARTICLE IV. — *Officers.*

The officers of this union shall be a president, three vice-presidents, secretary, and treasurer, whose duties shall be those usually belonging to such officers ; also six directors who, with the above officers, shall constitute an executive committee, having charge of all business not otherwise provided for. The officers and directors shall be chosen at each annual convention, and shall begin their terms of service at the close of the convention at which they are elected.

ARTICLE V. — *Meetings.*

(*a*) The executive committee shall arrange the time, place, and programme for an annual convention of this union.

(*b*) The executive committee may also provide for meetings of a part of this union, under a call for a district convention at such place and time as they deem best.

(*c*) The object of these meetings shall be instruction, inspiration, and fellowship, but not legislation. As this union cannot be held responsible for the fellowship of young people outside of the ranks of the Christian Endeavor societies, and in order that the union may not be used for partisan purposes, no delegate shall be appointed to other bodies, nor received from other bodies.

ARTICLE VI. — *Finance.*

The expenses of the union shall be met by the free-will offering of the societies, and no tax or assessment shall be levied upon the members.

ARTICLE VII. — *Districts.*

The executive committee may divide the State into districts, and appoint over each a district secretary, whose duties shall be to assist in organizing new societies when called upon, to report such new societies to the State secretary, and do what he can to arouse and increase the interest in Christian Endeavor work.

ARTICLE VIII. — *Amendments.*

This constitution may be amended by a two-thirds vote at any meeting of this union, provided notice of the proposed amendment was inserted in the call for that meeting, or was given at the previous meeting.

FORM OF CONSTITUTION FOR A LOCAL UNION.

ARTICLE I. — *Name.*

This Union shall be called the .... Christian Endeavor Union.

ARTICLE II. — *Object.*

The object of the Union shall be to stimulate the interest in societies of Christian Endeavor in .... and vicinity, to increase their mutual acquaintance, and to make them more useful in the service of God.

ARTICLE III. — *Members.*

Any society of Christian Endeavor connected with an evangelical church in .... and vicinity, whose constitution in its aims and prayer-meeting obligations conforms generally in spirit to " The Model Constitution," may join this union by notifying the secretary and upon approval by the executive committee.

ARTICLE IV. — *Officers.*

The officers shall be a president, vice-president, secretary, and treasurer. The president, vice-president, secretary, and treasurer shall be selected from active members, and shall serve one year, remaining in office until their successors are elected. All the presidents of the Christian Endeavor societies forming this union shall be vice-presidents of this union. The president, vice-presidents, secretary, and treasurer shall constitute an executive committee to provide for the general interests of the union.

ARTICLE V. — *Lookout Committee.*

A lookout committee shall be appointed, whose duty shall be to organize new societies wherever possible, to bring new societies into the union, and introduce them to the work, and to encourage and help the weaker societies as opportunity offers.

ARTICLE VI. — *Meetings.*

This society shall hold meetings at such times and places as may be determined by the executive committee. The president may call special meetings of the executive committee when he may deem it necessary.

ARTICLE VII. — *Duties of Officers.*

The duties of the president, vice-president, secretary, and treasurer shall be the duties usually pertaining to these offices.

ARTICLE VIII. — *Finance.*

The expenses of the union shall be met by the free-will offerings of the societies, and no tax or assessment shall be levied upon the members.

ARTICLE IX. — *Amendments.*

This constitution may be amended by a two-thirds vote of all the active members present at any regular meeting, the amendment having been submitted in writing, and notice having been given at least two weeks before action is taken.

Local Changes. — Two important features of the above constitutions are urged upon all unions, namely, the restrictions as to membership, which alone can make the unions homogeneous and effective, and the mode by which the expenses of the union are to be met, *i.e.*, by free-will offerings. Only one local union committee is provided for; similar articles should be added for the other committees desired. The composition of the executive committee, both of local and State unions, varies greatly, and several modes of formation are suggested in this manual.

Union Divisions. — Our large city unions have found it necessary in almost every case to form subdivisions which hold frequent gatherings, the entire

union coming together only once or twice a year.
The obvious mode of subdivision is by localities,
such as the North Side, South Side, and West Side
divisions of Chicago, and the district divisions of
New York. In addition, it may be necessary, as in
Philadelphia, which has its German Christian Endeavor Union, to make divisions based upon language. These divisions have their own sets of
officers, closely affiliated, of course, with the central
officers of the union.

Get a Supply. — In a good many local unions,
very few members have a printed copy of the constitution. The mistake is usually made of not getting
enough of these printed at the beginning to last for
a series of years. There are many savings that do
not pay, and this is one of them.

CHAPTER III.

THE PRESIDENT.

IT is important that the president of the Christian Endeavor local union should be a good speaker, but it is far more important that he be a good executive. Fortunate indeed the local union whose presiding officer combines these powers.

If I were asked to name the two qualities most useful for the president of a local union, I should say, good sense and good humor. With these, he will be master of the situation. Of course I am taking it for granted that he is a person of deep consecration, whose life, with all his powers and possessions, time, energies, thoughts, and plans, are wholly given up to his Master. He will need quickness of decision, ingenuity, industry, force. He should be fertile in expedients, and persistent in carrying them out. But above everything, he should be consecrated, and in the school of consecration he will learn what else he needs.

A Work of Oversight. — The most important work of the local union president is not what is very often held to be the most important, namely, the presiding at the public meetings, together with the preparation for them; it is the visiting of the local

societies. Each one of them should be visited in
turn, and as frequently as possible. Modestly let the
president of the union come in, and take part in the
meetings briefly, as any other Endeavorer, telling
the society, however, who he is, and bidding them
God speed in their work.

On these visits the president should use his eyes.
Let him note every good feature in the conduct of
the society. Let him observe, also, all the defects.
In fine, let him get as clear an idea of the society as
he can, in order to help the society.

This help is to be given in the meetings of the executive committee, before whom the president should
present the result of this systematic visitation of the
societies. He may discover a general lack in the
matter of prayer, or of cordiality toward strangers,
or of interest in the Junior work. Whatever it is
that he sees the societies to lack, he and the local
presidents, gathered together in the executive committee, should set themselves to remedying.

Nor should he forget to praise; and perhaps his
most valuable contribution to the executive committee meeting will be the account of helpful plans with
which he has become acquainted in the course of his
pilgrimage. These, through the presidents met together in the executive committee, he is enabled to
spread through the entire union.

A Friend. — The president's visits should put him
in close contact with all the workers. He should
meet them socially. He should take time to talk
with them both before and after the meetings. They

should come to know him as their friend, and should go to him for help and wise suggestions.

Above all, of course, he should avail himself of these visits to become a friend of the pastors. Let him learn from them whether their societies are doing all they could be expected to do, and let him make it plain to the pastors that the local union is their agency, seeking to be used of them along whatever lines of Christlike work they may wish to turn their Endeavorers to. Until the union president has put himself in this relation to the pastors, he cannot hope for success.

The vice-president should often accompany the president on his rounds, but more often he should lessen the president's work by going alone and reporting to him all incidents and observations.

Visiting Committees. — Just as one of the chief duties of the president of a local society is to visit the meetings of the committees of his society, — not so frequently as to make them think that he does not dare trust them alone, and yet often enough so that they will feel his continued interest in them, and so that he will keep in complete touch with the work of the whole society, — so one of the chief duties of the president of a local union is to visit the meetings of the union committees, especially the lookout committee, of which he should be a member *ex officio*, as the president of a local society is a member, *ex officio*, of his lookout committee. He should work closely with the president of the Junior union of the town, and should be *ex officio* member of the executive committee of that union.

State Presidents. — Similar suggestions may be made to the presidents of State unions. In every way these should seek to put themselves in close touch with the Endeavorers of the State, and especially with the pastors. The county unions need the help and inspiration of the State president. He should visit as many of these as possible. It will help the cause greatly if he can, once in a while, cross the State line and attend the Christian Endeavor gatherings of other States, carrying to them fresh enthusiasm in his every word, and bringing home again almost the zest of a trip abroad. Too few State presidents make interstate Christian Endeavor journeys.

By a correspondence as wide as his time and strength and other duties will permit, the State president will make himself the trusted friend and confidant of the State and county officers in all their Christian Endeavor perplexities and triumphs. The pastors throughout the State will come to know him as one that has deeply at heart the interests of Christ's kingdom, and is seeking to be their servant and the servant of the churches.

Well Informed. — Both State and local union presidents, in order to be worthy of the great trust confided to them, must keep up to date on the movement at large, must know how societies are being formed in lands across the sea, and what new methods have been tried and proved by the societies of our own land. They should read the best Christian Endeavor publications with much care. They should correspond with other union presidents, or, if time is lacking for that, they should get their union secretaries to correspond with the secretaries of other unions, and get from them full accounts of the plans found most helpful in other communities.

It is the duty of the president to circulate Christian Endeavor information in all wise ways. Of course, whatever Christian Endeavor literature is sent to the societies should be sent with the consent of the pastors.

All depends on whether the president tries to do it all himself, or remembers that he is simply to preside over the doings of others. If he confines himself to inspiring and directing the labors of those under his charge, he will not only do far more good to the cause, but he will do it far more easily and happily.

All this without mentioning what many people think the main business of the union president — the making of a convention programme and the presiding over the convention. And yet I would not convey the impression that I consider of slight importance these meetings in which so much lasting good is done, and from which so many thousands of noble young people get impulses toward the eternal life. Indeed, an entire section of this book is devoted to this subject, and little need be said about it here.

Planning the Convention. — To be a success, a convention — whether local union or State union — must be planned out carefully, and long before it comes off. Conventions are helpful in proportion as they are prayed over and thought over beforehand.

Have method in your convention. Know what you want and expect it to teach. Have definite results you count on to come from it.

Introduce as many strong features as you can, taking care, however, to avoid confusion, and to leave upon the Endeavorers a clear and abiding impression. In particular, make all your arrangements long before the convention, so as to avoid, as far as possible, that bustling around the platform that mars so many gatherings, and takes the point from so many noble addresses.

Managing a Convention. — A few words about conducting a convention. Think over the programme beforehand. Taking the topics and speakers one by one, plan the points you will make in introducing each speaker and in closing each discussion. Half of an address or debate or open parliament is in the introduction, and good introductions do not come impromptu. In this part of the presiding officer's work the chief necessity is good humor. No, there is one thing more important still, and that is brevity. A good president will occasionally sum up and emphasize a good address, and clinch it so tightly in the memory that everybody will carry away its main points; and he will do it in a sentence.

Keep order. *Keep order.* Do not for a moment allow a few ill-bred chatterers or restless aisle-trotters to cheat half the assembly of the good they have come for. Be a regular autocrat. The best presiding officer I ever saw out-czared the czar. Between the addresses he gave ample opportunity for getting

up and going out, but if there was the least disturb-
ance during an address, his threatening gavel was
shaken at the offender, and, if necessary, the speaker
was stopped and a public rebuke administered, followed by the delighted applause of the audience.
All this was done with a rare good humor that speed-
ily won the hearts of the great assembly — the largest body of teachers convened up to that time in
the history of the world.

Minimize business. Get your committees ready
beforehand if possible. Keep on time. If a speaker
is not there when he should be, do not wait for him,
but shift the programme so as to keep things mov-
ing, and quietly send a picked force of able-bodied
Endeavorers after the delinquent.

And finally — for some end must be made of a
really interminable matter — never forget that you
stand toward your speakers in the relation of host.
It is yours to make them feel at home. Put them
at the start on good terms with their audience. Win
for them a warm reception. At the close of their
address, say a few words of honest appreciation, and
show that you mean them. This is only the reward
that is their due.

Union Mottoes. — The president of the union will
impart a good deal of inspiration to the year's work
by proposing for it a definite motto such as the three
set before Pennsylvania societies one year. They
were: " One thousand new societies this year; "
" One soul saved for every member; " " More spiritual power in conventions and societies." These

mottoes should usually be briefer than the forego-
ing, and they should always express some definite
purpose.

The Ex-Presidents. — Many local and State unions
fail to utilize after the close of their term of office the
experience of the past presidents.   They should always be brought into definite and close connection
with the work of their successors.   An advisory
board might be formed, consisting of the ex-presidents of the union, but it is probably a better plan
for the ex-presidents to be members of the executive
committee for three years after the close of their
terms of office.

Overlapping. — Care should be taken that the secretaries of the various districts into which the State
may be divided are appointed some time before the
election of a new State president.   This is in order
that the State officers may begin their work with the
advantage of local assistants and correspondents who
have had some experience and training.

CHAPTER IV.

THE VICE–PRESIDENT.

THE chief exhortation regarding the office of vice-president should be made to the president, who is urged to make constant use of this officer, who is too often permitted to remain a nonentity. He should aid the president in the matter of visiting the societies and in carrying out his plans, as is insisted on in the section regarding the president. He should know the president's work as well as the president himself, and in fact, in the ideal union, the vice-president will be, during his entire term of office, in training for the presidency, and will be thought of as the president's natural and almost inevitable successor.

For this purpose let the president once in a while get the vice-president to preside at the meetings of the executive committee and at the mass meetings, even though he himself may be present.

Denominational Vice-Presidents. — Every State union should recognize the denominations that compose it, and the best way to do this and promote the growth of Christian Endeavor in these denominations is by the appointing each year of one vice-president from each denomination.

These denominational vice-presidents should be well distributed over the State, and they will form a splendid cabinet of officers for the president. They will be the natural leaders of Christian Endeavor work in their districts.

CHAPTER V.

THE SECRETARY.

OF course, the duty of the union secretary, as of all secretaries, is to keep a record of all business transacted by the union. He should also be the secretary of the executive committee. His reports of the union meetings should be far removed from the ordinary dull routine. They should have literary qualities. They should be bright and attractive, and make everybody that hears them wish he had been present at the meeting .described, if he was not.

Besides this, the union secretary should get returns from all the societies in the union, giving certain statistics. Those most commonly desired are the number of members of all classes, the number of accessions to each class during the year, the number of Endeavorers that have joined the church during the year, the societies' gifts to missions and in what direction they have given, the names of the regular committees of the societies, the average society attendance on the regular church services, as well as any special features of interest connected with the work of the societies.

It is the secretary's business to write to the speakers selected to address the union meeting, and obtain their consent. He will put through the printing of the programme. It should be his work to correspond with the secretaries of other unions, obtaining some account of their most important plans and methods.

The State Secretary.—The work of the State secretary is the same in its general outline as that of the local union secretary, except that, instead of corresponding with each society, he gets his statistics from the heads of county, district and city unions. His work during the convention is far from easy. He is often the timekeeper, and should accomplish his difficult task with tact yet with firmness, since the entire success of many a convention hinges upon the timekeeper. Then it is he that makes the announcements, and for this he must muster a voice like a fog-horn.

Suggestion Sheets. — These suggestion sheets should be prepared by the secretary of the union, and they will be equally valuable whether prepared by the State secretary to be sent among the secretaries of the district and county unions, or by the latter officers to be distributed among the local societies. These suggestion sheets are sent out with notices of conventions and State and district Christian Endeavor work. In each issue a request is made for new plans and ideas, to be given wider circulation in later suggestion sheets. Here is a sample suggestion sheet that came from Massachusetts : —

The missionary committee arranges a missionary meeting once a month. Africa is to be the subject of a series of talks. The first was geographical in its nature. A map drawn by one of the members was used. — *North Church, New Bedford.*

A society of New Bedford has a " glad-to-see-you committee." The name explains its object.

The Winslow Church, Taunton, is opened every Friday evening for the promotion of sociability. The social feature of two of these evenings in each month is in charge of the Y. P. S. C. E.

At one time our pastor and several young men of our society promised each other that we would sit at various places in the room upon prayer-meeting night, and when the leader called for prayers we would respond, allowing no waste time, The same was also pledged in regard to testimonies. — *Middle Street Christian society, New Bedford.*

A conundrum social, held by the Second Congregational Society of Attleboro, afforded much pleasure. One hundred conundrums pasted about the room kept all busy for an hour.

The Secretary's Letter. — When the secretary, whether of a county or a State union, has occasion to write to the societies, let him remember that the fewer words he uses, the more likely he is to be heeded. It is the long, tedious communications that are read carelessly and are not likely to be brought before the society.

If you do not use a typewriter, take care to write with great plainness, especially when you come to your own signature. If you do not use a letter-head, state what office you hold, and give your address. Enclose a stamped and self-directed envelope when you expect a reply, unless you are writing to some one who you know has the interests of the cause at heart as much as you.

When you write to speakers asking them to address the convention, be sure you tell them that their expenses will be paid.

Christian Endeavor Circuits. — Some secretaries of district unions — and the plan is valuable for local unions, and, with certain obvious limitations, for State unions — make a practice once a year of visiting thoroughly and systematically every society in their field. Arrangements must be made beforehand for meetings to be held at the times most convenient for the secretary. There may be two meetings a day, — a union committee conference, and a public meeting in the evening.

To meet the expenses of such a trip, the societies will be glad to make a small contribution each. In no other way can the district worker gain so full a knowledge of the needs and *personnel* of the societies.

Christian Endeavor Maps. — Every union secretary should draw an outline map of his district, placing upon it dots representing each Christian Endeavor society. In this way he can best get an idea of the portions of his district that require more work. He will know what places are most central for the holding of conventions. If the map is large enough to be seen over a good-sized room, it will be inspiring to add stars as new societies come into the union.

Pay Their Expenses. — When your union invites any one to make an extended address before it, you should take care that all his expenses are paid. If he is a Christian Endeavorer, he will not expect any further payment, of course ; but he has given in the preparation of the address far more than the union will give in money.

He may express a willingness to pay his own expenses, but it is better for the union to insist on paying them. When one gives many Christian Endeavor addresses, the expenses, though small in any single case, amount in the aggregate to quite a sum. This payment of expenses should be made as promptly as possible. Do not wait several days after the address before you attend to the matter.

CHAPTER VI.

THE TREASURER AND FINANCE

No officer of any Christian Endeavor union, local, county, or State, should receive any salary. That is a poor union, indeed, and greatly lacking in the spirit of Christian Endeavor, that cannot furnish young men and women to do this blessed work as a gift to the Master's cause. No dues should be levied, and, in general, little money should be required or expended. Some money is needed to pay the expenses of speakers, and to pay for programmes, postage, circulars, free literature for the spread of the movement, and other necessary expenses.

The small amount needed can usually be raised by collections at the public meetings. Where this is not sufficient, give the societies an opportunity to make voluntary offerings. This is best done through the executive committee, on which is some authorized member from each society. This committee knows just what will be needed, and in a few minutes the few dollars necessary can here be obtained.

The same remarks apply to the treasurer of the State union. All officers serve from love of the cause, and receive no pay. The small sum necessary to carry on the State work can be obtained by voluntary pledges made at the convention, or through the State executive committee.

One Way of Raising Money. — Notify the societies before the convention that their delegates will be expected to come prepared to pledge the society to pay a certain amount of money for the expenses of the union during the year. It will be better, of course, for the delegates to come with the money ready to hand it to the treasurer.

Establish in some central place a box with a slit in it, where these pledges can be deposited. The treasurer should be at an office at some convenient hour for the reception of money.

This is a straightforward and simple way of raising the little money needed for the union work, and it is the best way to adopt.

CHAPTER VII.

THE EXECUTIVE COMMITTEE.

THE executive committee of the local union should consist of the presidents of all the societies in the union. If it is a small union, there should also be from each society one or two delegates to be appointed by the society president.

The executive committee is to pass upon all matters of business before they are brought to the attention of the union. All communications should be referred to this committee by the secretary.

The Mass Meeting. — The meetings of the committee should be held at least as often as the mass meetings of the union, and at some time before. At these meetings the committee should decide upon the general plan of the coming union meeting; for instance, that the topic of Junior work shall be prominent, or that it shall be a missionary evening.

A sub-committee, on which should be some representatives from the church whose guests the union will be at the coming meeting, should be placed in charge of the programme. Let the members of the executive committee feel free to give suggestions to this sub-committee regarding the speakers or topics. The president of the union should, of course, be one of the members of this sub-committee, and the secretary of the union should be another.

A Discussion. — At the meeting of the executive committee, the president or some earnest Endeavorer should present a paper or make a short address touching upon some practical topic connected with the work of the union. This paper should be followed by a discussion or open parliament, whose theme may be connected with the address just listened to, or may be some general topic like " The needs of my society," or " The best plan recently carried out by my society." It would be well to have the chairman of the committees that are to report at the coming union meeting read their reports at the executive committee meeting, for criticism and suggestions.

The members cᶠ ᵗhe executive committee should represent the union in their own societies. They should seek to get the members of the society to attend the union meetings, should report those meetings to the society for the benefit of non-attendants, and should push through the societies the practical recommendations of the local union, as well as the annual calls of the union for financial support.

Report the Executive Committee Meeting. — Not unfrequently it happens that some societies are not represented at the executive committee meeting of the local union. It is precisely these societies that are likely to be in greatest need of the inspiration and

practical guidance of the committee meeting. Some
one should be deputed to report this meeting before
the society not represented. If this is not practicable,
the president of the union or the secretary should
write a letter containing a summary of the most important doings of the executive committee, and this
letter should be sent to be read before the societies
that were not represented.

An Advisory Board. — Local unions will gain
strength and stability if they appoint advisory boards
composed of the pastors of the churches represented
in the union, and, if the union is small enough to
make it wise, of one church officer from each church,
in addition. Before this board should be laid all
matters relative to aggressive methods of work before
the plans are adopted and put into active operation.

The appointment of this advisory board will emphasize the fact that Christian Endeavor respects church
authorities, and is in all points subordinate to the
church. It will prove a safeguard against jealousy
on the part of church officers, and against error on
the part of the young people, who frequently pos-
sess more zeal than knowledge. Best of all, it will
make the union more efficient, because its officers
will be brought in constant touch with the leaders
of Christian work in the community.

State Executive Committee Meetings. — Do you
find it hard to get full attendance at the meetings of
the State executive committee? Try the Ohio plan.
In that progressive State union the annual meetings
of the executive committee are held in connection

with conventions of large local or county unions, the programmes of which are made up of addresses from the able ministers of seventeen or eighteen evangelical denominations that make up the executive committee. This plan works exceedingly well.

CHAPTER VIII.

THE LOOKOUT COMMITTEE.

THE work of the union lookout committee corresponds closely in all details to that of the local Christian Endeavor society lookout committee. The president of the union should be a member *ex officio*, but should not be its chairman. It is best, unless the union is too large, to make the membership of the committee consist of the presidents of all the societies. In case any president is too busy to serve, let him appoint one of the most active members of his society to take his place. If the union is so large that this would make an unwieldy committee, then take pains to see that all sections of the city are well represented. Not all of the members of this committee should be young men. The counsels of the young women will also be needed.

The committee should meet certainly once a month, and when they are getting to work, at the beginning of the Christian Endeavor year, they should meet oftener.

A Reconnaissance. — The first thing for the union lookout committee to do is to take a survey of the field. In the ideal lookout committee each society will have a representative. Place before this representative the following questions, which may be added to as the chairman of the committee desires.

1. Have you a Junior Society of Christian Endeavor?

2. What standing committees has your society?

3. How much did you give last year to missions, and how was the money raised?

4. What per cent of your membership are young men?

5. What per cent of your members attend as a rule all the regular church meetings?

6. In what particulars are your members most likely to fail to keep the pledge?

7. How many associate members have you, and what use do you make of them?

8. How many of your active members are church members?

9. How many Christian Endeavor and denominational papers are taken in your society, and what are they?

10. What practical work is your society doing, such as relief work?

11. What committees that your society has not now do you think it needs?

12. What are some of the especial difficulties and troubles with which your society has to contend?

Require each member of the lookout committee to write out full answers to these questions, taking time to gather the facts. These reports should be handed in to the chairman on a certain date, and after he has had time to collate the information he should call a meeting of the lookout committee for the consideration of what these reports may disclose. He may see, for example, that there is a great need of united effort for the increase of the number of Junior societies in the union. He may see that the useful plan of the information committee is not appreciated by the societies of his town. He may see a great need of press committees, or of music committees. It may become manifest that very few of the members of the union are giving to missions systematically. The union may contain few associate members, or may be doing very little work for what associates it has. All of these the president will lay before the executive committee in a clear-cut report, backing up his statement with facts and figures 'aken from the reports of the members.

Utilizing the Facts. — Then will follow a discussion concerning ways and means of remedying the difficulties, or filling out the need. Suggestions for the next union meeting will be gained from this investigation. It may be best, for example, to occupy this entire meeting with a presentation of the Junior work — the blessedness of it and the need of it, the best Junior workers from the city and from neighboring cities being put in requisition. Sometimes only a single address at the union meeting, or an open parliament, may be enough. Or it may be sufficient to get from the United Society of Christian Endeavor literature on the subject, and distribute it throughout the societies. Or, if the need is a slight one, it may be met by private conversations or by letters. The mere fact that representatives of each society have been brought clearly to see the need will aid greatly in meeting it.

New Societies. — As the local lookout committee is concerned with the gaining of new members, so the union lookout committee has to do with the formation of new societies, and their admission to the union. Early in its year's work the committee will take a census of the churches of the city, discovering what churches are without Christian Endeavor societies, and in how many churches Christian Endeavor societies can probably be planted.

All work should be done with the coöperation of the pastors. After the facts are gained, certain members of the union lookout committee should call upon the pastors armed with literature and full information, and should endeavor to set before them clearly the advantages to be gained from Christian Endeavor societies. If you can interest neighboring pastors in the matter, you will find their aid most effective.

Organizing. — If the pastor desires to organize a Christian Endeavor society, the lookout committee of the union should offer to assist in the organization. If the offer is accepted, let the lookout committee appoint a delegation, consisting of the president of the union, or the chairman of the lookout committee, and a set of workers from the churches near by.

The young people of the church being gathered by invitation, a good speaker should explain to them the object of the society, the workings of the Christian Endeavor pledge and of the committees, and then proceed to organize, as explained in the United Society's leaflets regarding organization.

After the new society is formed, the lookout com-

mittee should propose to the union that it be admitted.   Their work does not by any means end
here, however.   The members of the committee
should visit the society often, consulting frequently
with its officers, and use every effort to introduce the
best methods and set the new society fully on its
feet.

Out Districts. — Lookout committees of local
unions have before them a wide and frequently entirely unoccupied field in the country districts, where
there are no churches, but where, with very little
effort, a Christian Endeavor society could be started.
These country societies, though small, do a blessed
work, and often constitute a nucleus about which a
church grows up.   This has been the history of not
a few useful churches throughout our land.

Besides this, the lookout committee should remember that the society finds one of its chief fields of
usefulness in schools, especially in seminaries, acade-
mies, and colleges.   Many of the young people here
gathered are Endeavorers when at home, but their
interest in the society and connection with its work
is likely to lapse sadly if there is no society in the
school where they spend the greater part of the year.
Of course, it is best if they will connect themselves
with the societies of some church where they sojourn,
but this is not always possible, and there is in almost
every school a fair opening for a union Christian
Endeavor society containing members of all denominations.   The union lookout committee should also
keep its eyes open for an opportunity of organizing

societies in orphans' homes, asylums, poorhouses, among railroad men, news boys, and similar classes that are too often neglected.

Evangelism. — Local unions can do a great deal of evangelistic work, and this falls appropriately within the province of the union lookout committee. Whatever is done here should be done with the fullest co-operation of the pastors, or not at all. In many communities the Christian Endeavor union has engaged an evangelist, and under its auspices union evangelistic meetings have been held, with the very best results. Sometimes the union undertakes missions in neglected portions of the city, either supporting a missionary, or itself carrying on missionary meetings.

In order that the lookout committee may keep posted regarding the field, they, as well as the president of the union, should make frequent visits to neighboring societies. They should keep themselves thoroughly informed, by careful reading of the literature of the United Society, regarding the best methods of society work.

Reports. — Special pains should be taken with the reports, through which, at every meeting of the local union, the lookout committee should present its plans and suggestions. These reports should be written by the best writer in the committee. They should be breezy and earnest and suggestive, and should, whenever they present an especially important point, be made the basis of an open parliament.

And the more complete and public are the reports

required from the societies composing a local union, the better will the work of those societies be likely to be. No society will be willing to present a record showing poor work. It has happened not seldom that when a public report was required of the societies, some of the societies begged for a reprieve, a postponement of investigation, until they could make a better showing. In a few weeks they were heard from with reports of more vigorous work.

Let the union lookout committee seek definite results, — not too many of them, but definites ones, — and then let it persevere until it gets them.

CHAPTER IX.

THE MISSIONARY COMMITTEE.

A Caution. — In undertaking union work outside of distinctive Christian Endeavor lines, such as missionary, good citizenship, evangelistic work, etc., great care should be taken to go so far and only so far as the pastors and churches approve. If any church is not willing that its society should enter upon any special work of this sort, the society should of course drop out, though in other lines it coöperates with the union.

There will be few occasions, I believe, when churches or pastors will object to their societies entering upon sensible and well-considered plans for the advancement of the kingdom, but they should always be consulted. For this purpose an advisory board of pastors, before recommended, is most desirable.

As to the composition of this committee, for large cities the Philadelphia plan is a good one. In Philadelphia, the union missionary committee consists of committees from each denomination, represented in the union, that cares to organize them. For example, the Presbyterians, Baptists, and Methodists have strong union missionary committees. The chief

officers of these denominational union committees
constitute the union missionary committee.

The denominational committees in Philadelphia
are thoroughly organized. For example, there is a
division that has charge of missionary lectures, obtaining missionaries from the denomination to address the societies and churches. Another division
zealously aims to keep the societies in touch with
the mission boards, and the boards with the societies. Another is an information sub-committee, and
stands ready to answer any questions, and to suggest methods of missionary study and activity. Still
another has charge of a magic lantern and sets of
slides bearing on mission fields, and is prepared to
give interesting missionary lectures whenever called
upon.

For Small Towns. — This plan, the ideal one for
a large city union, is, of course, out of the question
for small towns. Here the union missionary committee should be composed of the chairmen of the
local missionary committees, or of one member from
each society, when the chairman cannot serve.

Missionary Mass Meetings. — The work of the
union missionary committee is varied and exceedingly important. I will speak merely of some of the
endeavors that have actually been undertaken and
accomplished within my knowledge. The committee may get the societies to combine and obtain exceedingly fine missionary speakers for the purpose
of holding a union missionary mass meeting. These
mass meetings are of the greatest value though only

one meeting can be held, but in many places the entire Sabbath is made a missionary day, the pastors in all the churches that enter into the arrangement preaching missionary sermons in the morning, and conferences of missionary workers from all the societies meeting in the afternoon, presided over by the speaker of the evening, while in the evening, in some large hall, is held a grand missionary mass meeting, whose audience is composed of all the societies and congregations that join in the effort. No collections are taken up at these mass meetings, and the purpose is entirely to get and give inspiration. The cost of getting the speaker, which would usually be merely his expenses, is divided among the various societies.

Systematic Beneficence. — The union missionary committee should occasionally institute simultaneous efforts along the line of systematic beneficence. Collect statistics to find out how many tithe-givers there are in the different societies. Distribute leaflets, pointed and heart-searching, bearing on this matter. Appoint a night on which this subject shall be brought to the especial attention of the societies. Get each society, if possible, to appoint a special committee on systematic beneficence, for the purpose of agitation and personal work.

The union missionary committee may fittingly collect for the union secretary the statistics of the different societies in the matter of missionary giving, — how much each has given in the course of the year, to what objects it has gone, and in what manner the money has been raised. A banner may be offered by this committee to the society that contains the greatest proportionate number of systematic givers.

Missionary Information. — Much may be done by this committee to inspire the study of missions. They may urge the formation of clubs for this inspiring study. They may divide among the workers the missionary books in the public library for them to read and report on, making a list of those that prove especially attractive. This list may be distributed among the societies, and will serve as a guide to their use of the public library. If the public library is deficient in this branch of literature, the committee may have influence with the librarian and obtain new books.

A Union Collection. — It will help the missionary committees of the local societies if the union committee make a collection of missionary maps and curios from mission countries and pictures illustrating foreign customs and scenes, costumes, etc. This collection should be held by the chairman of the missionary committee, ready to be loaned to any society in whole or in part, as the needs of that society demand.

Union prayer meetings might fittingly be held on missionary topics. What more appropriate than that the union should pray over the debts of the missionary boards, or over some great crisis in missionary lands, like that in Japan and China caused by the late war, or that in Turkey caused by the Armenian massacres?

City Missions. — Much may be done by the union missionary committee to interest the Endeavorers in city missions. If there is no city missionary work, they may even undertake it themselves. It is entirely within the possibilities of a strong city union to open rooms in the slums of the city, where on every evening of the year there may be a refuge for the young men and women and the children. Here pleasant games may be found and interesting books and periodicals, and an occasional bright entertainment may be given, the societies taking turns in this service. Many city unions would readily furnish 365 young men and women to take charge, each for a night, or half that number to take charge for two nights each. Some unions have undertaken the work of making outdoor playgrounds for the poor children of the city; others of opening Sunday schools, or establishing classes in various useful studies and occupations.

But in many cities the union will be more useful if it co-operates with the city missions already established. In Boston, such co-operation in the case of one mission sends to that mission every night a delegation from some one of the city societies. Their bright songs, and fresh, hearty, sincere testimonies, have a strong and elevating effect on the degraded specimens of humanity brought together there. But the good the young people do in the work is far more than equalled by the good each one of them gets from it.

Whatever is said here of the union missionary committee applies as well, of course, to a county or district union as to a city union. Moreover, in the larger union also the work must be undertaken only with the consent cf the pastors of the societies engaged in it.

State Missionary Superintendents. — More and more the State unions are coming to appoint State missionary superintendents. The chief work of this officer is to co-operate with the union missionary committees of the districts, counties, and cities. Where these committees arrange missionary rallies, it is a great saving of money and time for the rallies of neighboring cities and districts to be held on such dates that eminent speakers can go from one town to another. Their expenses then rest lightly on any one community, and they can reach immense numbers of people with but little expenditure of time and strength.

Where the State is not provided well with these union missionary committees, the first work of the State missionary superintendent is, of course, to see that the unions appoint them. At the same time, the State superintendent should put himself in correspondence with the various boards, acquaint himself with their needs and their desires for the societies of their own denomination, and at the same time learn about as many accessible missionary speakers as possible.

CHAPTER X.

THE SOCIAL COMMITTEE.

THIS committee should be composed of one member from each society social committee in the union. It is best for this member to be the chairman, but wherever this is not possible, let the chairman appoint some efficient and interested Endeavorer from his committee.

Neighborhood Socials. — One of the matters within the province of the union social committee is the social relation existing between societies in churches near to one another in the city. Sometimes the union social committee can suggest the holding of neighborhood union socials in which near-by Endeavor societies unite. Those of two or three churches will be enough.

Denominational Socials. — Denominational socials, wherein all the Baptist Endeavor societies of the city meet together, or the Presbyterian, or the Congregational, or Methodist societies, are very pleasant occasions, and could be carried on under no more fit auspices than those of the union social committee. Besides, it would be profitable once in a while to hold union socials to which shall be invited only those Endeavorers that are at work along similar Christian Endeavor lines, as, for example, all the social committees of the union, all the prayer-meeting committees, and all the missionary workers of the union. Or, — and this would make a very profitable social, — all the associate members of the union, in company with all the lookout committees. At these socials appropriate exercises should be held, which would be a pleasure to devise, so many ideas would spring naturally to mind.

Socials at the Meetings. — But of course the main work of the union social committee must centre on the socials before and after the public meetings of the union. These should be in the hands of the members of the society in the church where the meeting is held, but the union social committee must be ready to give efficient aid. Their first duty will be to form the acquaintance of as many Endeavorers as possible, all over the city. Let them introduce themselves, if need be, and then introduce to one another those whom they have thus met. As the attendants on the union meeting arrive, they should be met at the door and given a hearty hand-shake. The union social committee, scattering themselves through the church, should try to establish pleasant conversations, and make all the attendants feel at home before the meeting begins. It is wonderful how much this will help the open parliaments and similar exercises that are to be held later.

Refreshments for Body and Mind. — Of course, the main social will be held at the conclusion of the formal exercises. Try to make a point to have these exercises so short as to leave at least half an hour before the time when the members must return to their homes. Entertaining societies may like to furnish refreshments. These should not be expensive, and should never go beyond, for instance, lemonade and wafers, or chocolate and cake, with sandwiches. For these refreshments the audience will be asked to adjourn to another room, and the social committee should promptly start the movement thither. While the members of the entertaining society are acting as waiters, let the social committee go for the wall flowers, and attempt to set all the Endeavorers to pleasant conversation. Get them to talking, if possible, about their committee work, their societies, and their churches. Especially bring the members up to the pastors and introduce them.

It is exceedingly important, therefore, that the members of the social committee should be on hand at every meeting of the union. The longer they continue in service, and the more meetings they attend in this way, the more valuable they will be to the union.

To Break Up Cliques. — The problem of preventing those that come to the union meetings from getting together into society cliques, and thus destroying the true fellowship of the meeting, may be solved in this way: Instruct the members of each committee to wear ribbons of the same special color. Thus, the prayer-meeting committee may wear blue, the lookout, white, the social, red, the flower, green, the missionary, purple, and so on.

At certain points in the meeting-room raise banners of these different colors, or cover the globes of the gas jets, if they are conveniently situated, with the appropriate colors, and require all to seat themselves under the light bearing their color. In this way workers from different parts of the city will be brought together, and will form pleasant acquaintances on the ground of their common interests.

The same plan may be utilized in the socials that follow the Christian Endeavor mass meetings, and, if refreshments are offered, there may be committee tables decked in appropriate colors, where the members of each committee may get their refreshments together.

Society Intervisitation. — Some unions keep in operation a very thorough system of society intervisitation, whereby, in the course of the year, each society will hold a union meeting with every other society, either in their own church or elsewhere. The schedule for this series of union meetings is carefully planned beforehand. Copies of the plan are made and given to the president of each society, who will see by the schedule just what nights of the year his society is expected to meet with other societies and what those societies are, telling him also when he may expect visits from other societies at his own church.

If the union is a large one, care should be taken not to make these visits so numerous as in any way to break into the regular habits of the Endeavorers, — their attendance on their own societies and church meetings.

Committee Visitation. — Sometimes the best plan of managing inter-society visitation is to provide for visits, not by single members, or by the societies as a whole; but by committees. The most appropriate committee is, of course, the lookout committee; and the union might arrange for visits by the lookout committees among neighboring societies. After this committee has become acquainted with the societies, the prayer-meeting committee might take its turn. But, as said before, these visits must be so arranged as not to cast any suspicion on the loyalty of the members to their own society and their own church, else they would better not be made at all.

Circular Letters. — In local unions where the scheme of inter-society visitation is not practical, or even in addition to that plan, it would be pleasant and helpful to establish a system of circular or "Round Robin" letters. Let the president of the union write a short, practical, stirring letter to the societies under his charge. This letter must be read before his home society, and let some one be delegated from this society to write a letter to go with it, in a certain fixed order, to a second society. Before this society let both letters be read, and a third be added in like manner.

When the letters have made the round of the union, and twenty, say, have accumulated, they will be handed to the president. He will detach his letter, write a new one, and add it to the pile. In this new letter he will comment on the series before him, emphasize the good suggestions, add fresh hints, and discuss the progress of the work since his first letter was written. This, with the twenty letters, will go before society No. 1, which, after detaching its own letter, reading the others, and adding a new contribution, will hand the correspondence to No. 2, and so on, until time shall end.

The advantages of these circular letters are manifold. Each society is put in touch and friendly rivalry with the whole body. Ideas quickly spread. Information is placed before the societies thoroughly and effectively. The leaders and the led are put in contact.

There are a few dangers. The letters must by no means take the place of frequent meetings together. The letters must never descend from a high plane of Christian love and humility to braggadocio and bantering. They may be bright and sometimes witty, but should never be burlesque or trivial. They should deal largely in ideas and plans, less in statistics, still less in complimentary personals. They should never be delayed in the hands of any society more than one week. Fresh hands should be given the work of writing the letter each time, that it may remain a pleasure, and not become a burden. Finally and chiefly, that the reading of the letters may not be a bore to the societies, they should be brief, brief, brief! They must be crisp and condensed. Of course the number of societies in the union would have much to do with the decision of this matter, but in most unions it would be best for each society to write a letter covering about ten pages of note paper, and then, putting the important matter into half a dozen sentences, destroy the ten pages !

Convention Reunions. — Often exceedingly pleasant friendships are formed among the attendants at the International or State Christian Endeavor conventions, and the officers of the union may, once a year, form a delightful social gathering of these, inviting, for example, all that have ever attended an International Christian Endeavor Convention to meet at a certain place to spend an evening together. Jovial addresses and cheerful conversation will make the time pass swiftly.

CHAPTER XI.

THE PRESS COMMITTEE.

THE work of the union press committee is so closely associated with the work of the press committees of the local Christian Endeavor societies that the union committee can scarcely proceed far until it has organized press committees in connection with each church. These local press committees should gather items from the church and Sunday school, as well as from the Christian Endeavor society.

There will, of course, be no vainglory in the matter. It will simply be the effort of the committee to see that the church, the most important institution in all the world, is, if possible, as well represented in the daily press as prize fights and shameful scandals.

The Local Committee. — The local press committee should do all its work in co-operation with the pastor. Every society contains members of literary ability and with some reportorial instinct, and these members should be utilized and kept in the service even though they chance to be on other committees also. See to it, however, that every local press committee has one or two inexperienced members upon it, in training to take up the work when the need shall call for them. The chairmen of these local press committees will constitute the press committee of the Christian Endeavor union.

Some Hints for Reporters. — The chairman of this union press committee should be a practical journalist, if possible. If he is not one, he should become one, learning thoroughly from some reporter or editor the ins and outs of newspaper work.

If he wants to make a success of his undertaking, he should learn, in the first place, that the fewer and shorter the calls he makes upon the editors, the better. The manuscript he hands in must be written on one side of the paper and in good black ink, with liberal spaces between the lines and about the edges. His paragraphing and punctuation and spelling must be faultless. Moreover, he must learn what amount of copy can be used, and never transgress the limits. He must know just when the copy is due, and must be as regular as the sun in handing it in. Above all, he must seek in the work of his committee to avoid dullness and monotony. No "pull" is needed to get his items into the papers, provided he manifests in his work the three virtues most dear to the hearts of editors, — "business," brevity, and brightness.

System — Co-operation. — If the union press committee is at work in a large city, the chairman of the committee should divide the papers of the city among the members of his committee, each of whom takes charge of the Christian Endeavor items going to one paper.

All news notes should be sent in from the local committees to the chairman, who arranges them, and makes himself master of their contents. Regularly all members of the committee should meet and should write up their notes together, using the material in the hands of the chairman. Never send the same item to two different papers; always change the form and manner of presenting it.

After the work is done, take some time for mutual criticism, and, whenever possible, present your work to experts for their judgment. Remember that whatever is worth doing is worth doing well, and the art of paragraph-making is among the most difficult of arts.

What to Report. — What kind of items is your committee to hand in? You may tell about the visitors among the families of your congregation, especially those of some importance. Make mention of the notable sermons of the city pastors, those especially that are strong spiritually. Once in a while quote some particularly pointed sentences, but no more than a sentence or two at a time. When the pastors exchange with men from other cities, note the fact. Whatever lectures are given in the different churches, whatever mission work is undertaken, whatever new plans for church work are formed, should be mentioned. Tell about the church socials, about the church mission work, the accessions to the churches, the good prayer meetings, the new officers, the Sunday school, and (of course) the Christian Endeavor society. Remember that the editor will especially appreciate advance notices of important church events that are to come.

Never put in anything for the purpose of filling up. If your committee cannot find enough items of genuine interest, you would better conclude that journalism is not your business.

Utilizing the Denominational Papers. — One great field of the union press committee is the denominational papers, and the press committee should be divided into sub-committees, one for each denomination represented in the city, made up of young people belonging to those churches. These will select from the material in the hands of the chairman only such items as will be especially pleasing and helpful in their denominational papers, and these they will write up as briefly as possible, taking pains to preserve the interest. Those members of the union committee that are not given special charge of the local city papers should be set over this branch of the work. Pains should be taken to report to the denominational papers all churches, and show no favoritism.

In sending items to the press, notice the form that is used in printing the items, and make your manuscript correspond to this form. Notice especially the kinds of items that are printed, and remember that these are an index of the editor's desires.

Local Union Papers. — I do not feel inclined to say very much about local union papers, for the reason that I do not believe very much in them, except, possibly, in some of our largest unions; and even there the local union paper should not take the place of press work in other directions. Long and thorough observation has convinced me that our Endeavorers are to a great extent wasting the money, energy, and time they put into local Christian Endeavor papers.

Local Christian Endeavor news can easily be inserted in the local newspapers, and this is a double gain : the cost is little or nothing, and the influence of the society is many times greater. Religious news is thus spread throughout the entire community, reaching non-Christians as well as Christians, while the local Christian Endeavor paper would go only to the Endeavorers.

I believe that if local union officers have special messages they wish to send to the societies, the best means is to send manifolded letters to the presidents, for them to read before their societies. Matters of general interest that your union wishes to get before the Christian Endeavor world at large are always welcome in THE GOLDEN RULE. Matters of denominational interest will be eagerly welcomed in the denominational journals.

Scrap-Books. — The union press committee should by all means keep a scrap-book of the work accomplished. This will be of increasing interest and value as your work goes on. But do not make the mistake some committees make of measuring your work by quantity rather than quality ; by the number of columns you get into the papers, rather than by the impression your paragraphs make and the results that can be traced to them. Do not be satisfied, either, with getting into inferior papers. Seek to obtain entrance into the columns of the very best. And above all, do not put up with inferior work in yourself or your subordinates. This is God's work, and it should have the very best talents you can command.

The Convention Press Committee. — One of the most important of the convention committees is the press committee. At the head should be a practical Christian Endeavor worker, and among its members should be stenographers and typewriters, besides those skilled in the use of the pen.

Bulletins should be sent out before the convention to all the prominent papers. These bulletins should tell the most important plans for the convention, and name the most important speakers, giving interesting biographical facts. As the time for the convention approaches, the bulletins should be more frequent and longer.

Find out before the convention about how much space the different papers will be likely to devote to the meetings, and obtain from the speakers, as far as possible, copies of their addresses. The press committee should make typewritten or printed copies of these addresses for the different papers, furnishing them abridged or unabridged, as the space at their command would indicate, remembering that each paper will wish to cover the entire ground, however limited may be the space.

See that the reporters' tables are conveniently

placed, furnished with programmes, and with all needed facilities. Set before them as the sessions proceed the abstracts or the full copies of the speeches that you have prepared, or, if desired, send them to the offices in time for them to be put into type beforehand.

On the morning of the opening of the convention see that the papers contain as much general information regarding the movement as you can get them to print. The literature of the United Society will furnish abundant material.

The work of the press committee should be continued after the close of the convention, and the country papers and weekly papers will need to be followed up, pains being taken to have the gatherings reported in these as fully as possible.

CHAPTER XII.

THE MUSIC COMMITTEE.

THE chairmen of the local societies' music committees will properly constitute the union music committee. Our societies do not form-music committees so commonly as I wish they might. A great field is open before Christian Endeavor societies along this line of training for better congregational singing.

One of the most obvious duties of the union music committee is to form a union choir. A good leader may easily be obtained, who will give his services for love of the work, and the young people will gather in large numbers to get the advantage of this excellent training, and because of the pleasure the singing will give. The union choir will add vastly to the attendance on your union meetings and to the interest of the services, and besides, it is neither just, nor always profitable, to depend for the music of your union meetings upon the choir of the church whose hospitality you are receiving.

The union music committee may provide solos, quartettes, and the like, for the union meetings, but do so sparingly, for choruses should be the main dependence.

In the Societies. — Do not fail to make the influence of the committee felt in the direction of better music in the local societies. Through this committee push all plans productive of this result, such as the plan of committing to memory one hymn a month, the plan of hymn consecration in our consecration meetings, the plan of hymn socials, etc. Urge the Endeavorers to utilize their hymn-books wholly, not confining themselves to a few familiar songs, and constantly hold before them the noble object of improving the congregational singing of the future.

State Hymns. — Many State unions now have their hymns that are sung with increasing fervor by the delegates, as the years go on, and as many precious memories cluster about the songs. So much is to be made of these State hymns, not only in the State but in the International Conventions, that the very greatest care should be taken in adopting them. The ability to write a good song, one appropriate in sentiment and bright in movement, and at the same time full of poetic feeling, is exceedingly rare. Some State hymns are lamentably weak in all these respects, and should be discarded and replaced by others more dignified and beautiful. Our unions have a responsibility for cultivating the good taste of their members, and the constant singing of doggerel will do much to disgust, not only the Endeavorers, but all that hear them.

It might be well to hold a public competition,

presided over by the best writers of your State, men and women of national reputation. Let the competition last for many months, if need be, and accept no hymn finally that does not receive the unanimous approval of your committee of judges.

CHAPTER XIII.

THE CHRISTIAN–CITIZENSHIP COMMITTEE.

THE work of this committee varies greatly, according to the size of the place in which the union is situated. Its membership consists of one at least from each society, and it is better, as our suffrage laws now stand, that this committee should consist solely of the older young men.

Not in Politics. — One caution should be emphasized at the beginning of these suggestions, and that is, that the Christian citizenship committee should under no circumstances have anything to do with partisan politics. Politics in the abstract they *must* touch, or they will accomplish nothing, but their work must always apply to all parties equally, and be confined chiefly to studies in preparation for citizenship.

Addresses. — The work of instruction, however, is always appropriate. The union might well obtain Christian citizenship lectures from some citizen distinguished alike for practical acquaintance with public affairs and for sound morality. A set of most helpful addresses might be arranged, for example, whose general purpose would be to inform the Endeavorers regarding the fundamental outlines and conditions of their city government. For example, one well-informed man might speak, on some week-day evening, about the city streets, the board that has charge of them, the conditions of cleanliness and of convenience, and the errors in the present management of them. In a similar way the question of the municipalization of gas manufacture or of street car lines might be taken up, or the fire department or the police department might be discussed. It would be especially helpful to call in some prominent worker in the city charities, and ask him to explain them. There is lamentable public ignorance on the question of temperance laws. Many of us do not know what the laws are, still less whether they are being enforced, and a practical statement of these laws by a Christian lawyer would constitute a profitable evening. The school laws and the condition of the public schools furnish another important topic. If you are in a county, rather than a city, union, the field is almost as extensive. You can study the condition of your township, its poorhouses and poor laws, its jails, its schools and school laws, and the temperance problem.

Studying Citizenship. — The Christian-citizenship committee of the union may well organize classes of Endeavorers for the study of some of the many admirable books on Christian citizenship that have recently been published. A competent teacher would quite readily be found in any community, and these classes, though they might be small, would consist of the very cream of the young citizenship, those most likely to influence events in future.

Down in Black and White. — I know of no better educational work a committee could undertake than the preparation of a good-citizenship map of the city, — a map, for instance, on which might be drawn all the saloons, the map being colored to represent the political complexion of each district; a map on which the number of arrests, within a certain time, from each district might be represented, the number of murders and other crimes committed in different portions of the city, etc. Such charts would be of inestimable value to the young citizens, and those from distant cities might be exchanged and studied.

Eye-Witnesses. — Another method is to divide the field that it is proposed to study among the different societies, assigning to each society one portion of the field, to be thoroughly studied and reported upon by the best speakers of the society at a union meeting. One society, for instance, might take the city council and its work; another, the mayor, his powers, and how they have been used; another, the city papers and their influence; another, the Sabbath, and how it is kept in the city, together with a study of the laws pertaining to the Sabbath. These reports, if carefully prepared, would in themselves constitute the best of material for union meetings. They should always be followed by open parliaments.

Be Modest. — Many of these discussions may bring

out evils in the city government, but the young people should remember that it is foolish in them to attempt to suppress them alone. They need older heads for guidance and support. Whatever is done in the direction of political reform we can expect to come only from citizens' movements and reform leagues, manned by experienced Christians. Endeavorers will always throw themselves heart and soul into such movements and organizations. Our work is to study and prepare ourselves to take the lead in precisely such movements.

I do not see, however, any harm in the circulation of petitions, and this affords a means of giving testimony which is all the Christian Endeavor union ought to ask, considering the age of most of its members. The union press committee can exert considerable influence along this line, if it uses with tact the space accorded it in the city papers.

Temperance Work.— Until the demon of strong drink has left the land, and left it forever, one of the most important of Christian Endeavor union enterprises will always be aimed at the abolition of the saloon. Many unions have obtained temperance evangelists and conducted courses of gospel temperance meetings, winning many pledge-signers, and converting drunkards to a life of sobriety and purity. In not a few places the Christian Endeavor unions have lent effective aid to no-license campaigns, in many of which the union has been the leader. By petition and in other ways several Christian Endeavor unions have been able to promote temperance legislation, and to bring about the enforcement of temperance laws already enacted. In all such endeavors, it need not be reiterated, the local union will go only in such directions and so far as the pastors of the churches are prepared to lead the way.

Pledges. — The circulation of Christian citizenship pledges is to be commended most heartily. These pledges, worded according to the desire of the union, should at least bind the one who signs them to investigate the character of all for whom he votes, to vote for none but good men, to study earnestly all matters pertaining to the city government, to throw his influence always on the side of the suppression of the liquor traffic, and, in general, to vote as he prays and pray as he votes.

CHAPTER XIV.

THE GOOD—LITERATURE COMMITTEE.

THE work of this committee depends upon the work of local good-literature committees. If these local committees do not exist, the good-literature committee of the union should consider it its first duty to form them.

Don't Throw It Away. — In all our churches a vast amount of admirable literature is going to waste, while in hundreds of thousands of homes and institutions this literature is greatly needed. It is the work of the union good-literature committee to see that this wasted food goes to the hungry mouths. There should be a regular day on which the bundles of books, magazines, and papers can be brought from the local societies to some central distributing place, where the union good-literature committee takes charge of them, divides and sorts them, and sends them where they can do the most good, to jails, hospitals, police stations, railroad station, boxes in the city parks, poorhouses, asylums, orphans' homes, and similar places.

A Useful Institution. — The Good-Literature Exchange of the Chicago Union, whose address is Box 1013, Chicago, Ill., is carrying on the useful work of

putting local unions and local societies in connection
with missionaries and institutions all over the country that may apply to them for good literature. Much
has already been accomplished, but very little com-
pared with what could be done if the local unions
were awake to the need and the opportunity.

The union committee should take note what societies are sending in this literature and what are
not, and should spur those that are lagging. They
should discover, by correspondence and observation,
the good that is being done by the literature that is
given out, and tell about it in their reports before
the local union, in order to encourage to still further
gifts.

Other Work. — Besides the gathering of literature
that would otherwise be wasted, it is within the
province of the union good-literature committee to
promote the circulation of good literature among
Christian Endeavorers and their families ; to gather
statistics of the missionary, denominational, and
Christian Endeavor papers taken among the Endeavorers ; and, where these are not taken in proper
quantities, to push the circulation of these indispen-
sable adjuncts to practical, earnest Christianity.

Find out whether the societies are appreciating
the inestimable value of tracts and missionary and
temperance leaflets, and, so far as you can, promote
the circulation and use of these swift-winged mes-
sengers of truth.

CHAPTER XV.

THE CORRESPONDENCE COMMITTEE.

UNLESS your union is a very large one, a single Endeavorer will suffice for the membership of the union correspondence committee. The work of the committee is to receive and send away notifications of intended changes of residence among Christian Endeavorers. If, for example, a member of a Baptist Christian Endeavor society of New York City intended to move to Chicago, he himself, or some friend for him, would notify the correspondence committee of the New York Union, who would write to the correspondence committee of the Chicago Union, telling him that on about such a date the Endeavorer would move to Chicago, and giving his Chicago address. It would then be the duty of the Chicago correspondence committee to pass the letter on to the president or secretary of the Baptist society nearest the future home of this Endeavorer. The lookout committee of this society would see that the Endeavorer had an earnest invitation to join society, Sunday school, and church.

A list of correspondence committees is kept at the headquarters, and if any Endeavorer wishes their services, the addresses are easily obtained. Much

good can be done by these committees. Young
people whose friends are anxious about their religious welfare are hunted up, and sometimes rescued
from surroundings that might have proved irresistible
temptations. Obviously, the correspondence committee should be permanent, if possible.

Boarding-house Bureaus. — A work that many a
Christian Endeavor union existing in a large city
might well undertake is the furnishing of suitable
homes to the young men and the young women that
come to the city from the country seeking employ-
ment. Scores of them are led into sin by being
obliged to take up their abodes in lodgings where
they meet with evil companions.

It will be easy for the Christian Endeavor union to
establish a central bureau where would be recorded
names of all church members who may be willing
to take young men or women into their homes.
Communication should be established with country
pastors and societies. This work of the union
should be as widely advertised as that of the correspondence committee, so that whenever a young
person leaves home for the city, his or her name
may be sent to the bureau. It at once sees that
a home is provided the new-comer with a family of
his own denomination.

CHAPTER XVI.

COMMITTEE CONFERENCES.

IN. speaking of the different committees of the union, nothing has been said about committee conferences, yet all of the union committees should hold them, and there should be conferences, also under the auspices of the union, for each of the committees of the local society unrepresented in the union organization, such as the prayer-meeting, flower, and information committees.

The Time. — These committee conferences should be held once a year, and among the first duties of the executive committee will be the formation of a schedule for the conferences. These conferences should be held in the order of their importance and timeliness. One for the prayer-meeting committee and another for the lookout committee, for example, should be held early in each Christian Endeavor year, and one for the missionary committee should come soon after.

The Place. — The committee conferences should be held in the various churches of the city. Let each meet in the church whose society contains the most efficient committee of the kind whose work is to be discussed. For instance, if a certain church has the best missionary committee of the union, hold at that church the missionary committee conference.

The Programme. — Each conference should be opened by a brief paper, inspiring, practical, and suggestive, or by several short papers treating different phases of the same topic; but always these papers should be followed by an open parliament, whose leader should not be the same one that presents the paper. It is well also to have a question-box, or, though this is not quite so valuable, an answer-box. These must be announced beforehand in order to be successful.

As a sample programme, take this for a conference of the social committees of the union: —

Paper on the spiritual side of social committee work.

Question-box.

An open parliament, whose leader will ask the audience to answer such questions as these: — What is the best social your society ever held? What is one of the new schemes your social committee has found valuable? How do you make strangers feel at home at your socials? What does your social committee do to add pleasantness to your prayer meetings? How do you raise money for socials?

A model social.

By Ticket. — There should be no attempt to seek an audience for these committee conferences. None but practical workers especially interested in the subject should be admitted. It is best to admit them all by ticket, and a certain number of tickets should be furnished each society. This number should be large enough to admit each member of the committee from that society, as well as, possibly, an equal number of interested friends.

District Conferences. — Sometimes it may not be practicable to hold committee conferences for all the societies of a large city union. In this case district committee conferences at least can be organized. To such conferences should be invited all the committee workers in two or three societies conveniently situated. Certain practical Christian Endeavor topics should be announced beforehand, and serve as the nucleus of the evening's discussions.

The union lookout committee would be the proper persons to preside over such a gathering. The topic may be opened by some member of the union lookout committee, who speaks for five or six minutes. Then follows a general practical discussion. Both written and verbal questions are answered, and especial effort is made to disclose clearly and positively the true Christian Endeavor principles. The societies bring up for discussion the particular lines of work in which each feels need of suggestion.

CHAPTER XVII.

VARIOUS USEFUL METHODS.

A Union Directory. — Every local union should have printed some sort of directory of the societies composing it. The directory may be no more extensive than a simple four-page leaflet, or by the use of advertisements it may be found possible to publish without loss quite a pamphlet. This directory should contain the date of organization of each society, the name of the first president, and possibly of succeeding presidents, the number of members on a certain date, the time of meeting, the church with which the society is connected, the Junior society, the name of the pastor, and similar information. There should also be an account of the union drawn up along similar lines.

How Often ? — As to the frequency of union meetings, it is my opinion that once in three months is usually often enough. Every union meeting should present one strong speaker and address, and one is enough. Give him plenty of time. Put in one open parliament, question-box, answer-box, or discussion, — something to draw out all the Endeavorers present, closing with a brief consecration meeting, and you have, in my opinion, an ideal union meeting. The open parliament may discuss some general topic such as, " The greatest need of my society," "The best plan my society has recently carried out," and the like ; or the topic may be connected with the theme of the prominent speaker of the evening.

A Report Meeting. — An admirable local union meeting might consist of nothing but reports from the presidents of the different societies, these reports being limited in length to five minutes, and being followed by a discussion of their salient points, in which the entire audience will participate.

Choosing Officers. — Christian Endeavor conventions should be one place in the universe where the last are promoted, and those who would be first made to take back seats. Let the office seek the man, and never the man, or the man's friends for him, seek the office.

One other bit of advice. It is well to represent in the list of officers all sections and denominations, but this should not be the main idea kept in mind. Your chief purpose is the efficiency of the union; choose men best adapted to promote this. If all other interests can also be well represented, so much the better.

The Nominating Committee. — To avoid suspicion of favoritism, the nominating committee should be named, not by the president, but by a committee consisting of the delegates of different churches, if it is a local union, or from different sections, if it is a State union. When the president names the nominating committee his choice is likely to be limited to his personal friends, and as good a committee will not result as if the wisdom of many from different sections contributes to the selection.

Flags. — Gradually the State unions are adopting colors, and the local unions are doing the same, though more slowly. The Philadelphia. Union is seeking to introduce throughout the Christian Endeavor world the custom of carrying flags of uniform size, whose colors shall be characteristic of the State and local unions. The flags are to be about seven by nine inches in size, and are to contain no lettering or design. They are simply for the display of colors, those of Pennsylvania being dark red and dark blue, half and half. Above the flag is a pennant to show the colors of the city union, those of Philadelphia being light blue and white.

These flags may be mounted on jointed poles that can easily be carried in the pocket. They will serve as rallying points for delegations at Christian Endeavor conventions, and the waving of these flags will make a very beautiful salute, as good as the Chautauqua.

Banner Societies. — Recognize once a year by the presentation of a local union banner the society that during the year has added the largest number of active members in proportion to the membership it had at the beginning of the year, at the same time showing an attendance at the consecration meeting and participation of the members in it equal to the average of the union. Call this the " banner evangelistic society." Give another banner to the society that contributes the largest amount of money to its church and to home missions, in proportion to its membership, while at the same time it contributes to foreign missions an amount equal to the average contributed by the societies of the union. This will be called the " banner missionary society."

Attendance Banners. — It is the custom in many unions to call the roll of the societies at the beginning, or sometimes at the end of the programme. As the societies composing the union are called, the members present from each society rise, and an assistant to the secretary counts their number. Sometimes a banner is given to the society, other than that entertaining the union, which sends the largest delegation. This banner is carried by the society to the next local union meeting, and either retained or handed over to some more successful society.

Some unions may like to know the custom of the Essex County, N. J., Union, which presents semi-annually to the society which has to its credit the largest aggregate attendance on union meetings, a handsomely engraved certificate, and another to the society that has the largest attendance in proportion to membership. The statistics, of course, are obtained by reports from each society to the secretary of the union

CHAPTER XVIII.

BEFORE AND AFTER THE CONVENTION.

Prayer for Conventions. — All our conventions should be preceded by earnest prayer for them, offered by the local societies involved. Let the announcement of the convention include a call for such prayer, and, that it may be a true concert of prayer, let it all come upon the same day. This call should enumerate the particular features of the convention for which prayer is especially desired.

Convention Delegates. — A good way to raise money to send delegates to the Christian Endeavor convention is to distribute ballots like the following to the members of the society.

I DESIRE TO SEE

....

a delegate from the Christian Endeavor society of the First Baptist Church to the International Christian Endeavor Convention to be held at Cleveland next July. I send one cent and cast one ballot for the above candidate.

Any one can cast as many ballots as he pleases, provided the one cent accompanies the ballot. If enough is received to pay the expenses of more than one, the two that receive the largest number of votes will be sent.

Sometimes a lecture or a special entertainment may be given for the raising of money to send delegates. The tickets for this entertainment may be divided into two parts by perforation. One of these parts is a ticket of admission, while the other is a blank vote to be filled out by the purchaser with the name of the Endeavorer whom he would like to send to the convention as the society delegate.

Or, it may be found advantageous to devote the latter half of some prayer meeting to this matter of raising money. Let the leader speak earnestly of the plan, and the good to be gained by delegate representation, urging every one to give something, but to make the amount a matter between God and his conscience. While they all bow their heads in silent prayer, the ushers pass quietly around and present the subscription papers.

A union savings-bank may be established in the case of International Conventions, whereby the members of the union may save up their money for the purpose of going to the Convention. Payment of ten cents will open an account. Deposits are to be made in sums of not less than one dollar. Regular receipts are given and bank books kept. The earnings from the interest may go to the union and be used for its expenses.

By the way, the best delegate to send will be your pastor. If he is going anyway, take pains to select some Endeavorer whose report will be a genuine inspiration to the society.

Christian Endeavor Excursions. — It is always best, in order to avoid confusion, for the State union to manage, through a regularly appointed officer, the State excursion to the International Convention. Sometimes, through failure to attend to this matter in good season, rival excursions are organized and bad feeling may result, as well as a division of the forces and the enthusiasm of the State.

Let it be understood that any money made out of the excursion shall go to the State treasury for the work of the State union, though, of course, when a busy man takes time from his business to manage such a complicated affair, it is only right that he should receive some compensation for his services. The accounts of the excursion manager should be audited and reported in the same way as those of the treasurer.

Delegates' Certificates. — A convenient delegate's ticket to be presented by all attendants at the convention, may be arranged in this way. After an appropriate head, let it read:

This is to certify that ....is a member of the Y. P. S. C. E. of the .... church, at..........
....

(Signed) ....

President or Secretary.

A footnote will tell to whom the ticket is to be handed on arrival at the convention city. On the back are directions for reaching the convention building. A perforated stub is marked to be filled out and sent, as soon as the ticket is received by the Endeavorer, to the chairman of the entertainment committee in the convention city, his address being given. The stub will read:

Name..

Address...

When expected to arrive........................by the............ railway.

Do you desire entertainment?................................

If you desire to room with some particular person, please note the name...

(*Please prefix to your name Mr., Mrs., or Miss.*)

Conventions in Succession. — The presidents of State unions may often time their conventions in such a way as to permit strong speakers to go from one convention to another, thus economizing the money paid for fares and the time of the speaker, and enabling the conventions to command the services of the very best speakers. By a little previous correspondence, such convention tours may be arranged by the State presidents for the brightest and most helpful speakers in the Christian Endeavor world.

Greetings. — The pleasant custom of sending greetings from one State convention to another is happily growing of recent years. These messages always add much to the interest of the convention, and strengthen that " tie that binds our hearts in Christian love."

If the message is sent by mail some time before the convention, it can be more extended and attractive. If a telegram is sent at the time of the convention, the best way is to refer to a Scripture verse that will express ʹthe sentiment desired to be conveyed.

Scan carefully the list of conventions given in THE GOLDEN RULE that are to be held at or near the date of your own, and let the proper officers send them these brotherly greetings.

Con vention Reports. — It will be found that only the largest State unions can successfully publish a report of the State convention. The cost is considerable, and to sell an edition requires much business ability. Moreover, no slight editorial skill is needed to prepare for profitable reading a summary of a crowded convention. Nevertheless, in some States this has been done, and well done. With the aid of advertising, such reports can easily be made to sell for ten cents. If they are persistently advertised at the time of the convention, a large number of the delegates will subscribe for them.

These reports not only furnish a valuable record of the work done during the convention, but constitute good campaign literature for use during the coming year. There should be, by the way, a wider mutual exchange of reports among the officers of State unions.

Where the pamphlet report is not found practicable, the newspaper report may be used for spreading the influence of the convention. Usually this will prove, on the whole, the most advantageous course.

Echo Meetings. — After every State and national convention, the local union should hold an echo meeting. It is not necessary, of course, to devote the whole evening to reminiscences of the convention, but a convention flavor may be given to the programme. Especially after the International Conventions these echo meetings are pleasant and profitable.

If the convention adopted, as the International Conventions do, any special colors, these may be used in the decoration of the room where the echo meeting is held. Songs characteristic of the convention should be sung. Of course, the returned delegates should speak, but opportunity should be given also for others to state what they have gleaned from newspaper accounts, and the accounts in THE GOLDEN RULE. Sometimes when no delegates from the union attended the convention, a good echo meeting can be made up from these printed reports alone.

If there are many returned delegates, the leader of the evening may divide the report, and ask carefully selected persons to speak on separate topics. Some one, for example, who has a good imagination and clear use of language, should describe the meeting places, the coming of the delegates, and other stirring scenes. Some one with a keen sense of humor may describe the comical as well as the pathetic incidents. Some practical worker may give an account of the new ways of working learned at the convention. Some spiritually minded Endeavorer will speak of the consecration meeting, and the evangelistic effect of the gathering.

Reporting Bands. — Suggest to the attendants on State Christian Endeavor conventions, as well as to those that go to the international gatherings, that they organize themselves on their return into reporting bands, that go around visiting less fortunate societies, and presenting in bright ways an account of their convention experiences.

CHAPTER XIX.

CONDUCTING A CONVENTION.

Merely Mass Meetings. — You will avoid many a pitfall if you understand clearly, from first to last of your convention management, this wise and necessary Christian Endeavor principle, that our conventions are mass meetings, pure and simple. They are not delegated bodies. They have no legislative functions. They levy no taxes, issue no commands. They are for purposes of inspiration solely. Along this line your convention will prove fruitful. Leave everything beyond it to the home churches and the pastors.

Be Prompt. — Too much can scarcely be said about the supreme importance of promptness in carrying on Christian Endeavor conventions. This is not merely for the good of the speakers, who are too often cheated out of time that properly belongs to them, and for the good of the audience, whose younger members should not be kept away from their homes too late, but especially on account of the training Christian Endeavor work should give for the conduct of life. A slovenly manner of carrying on the Christian Endeavor meetings is sure to produce slovenliness in all our work.

The programme should be so constructed as to leave ample spaces for all business. The reports of committees, announcements, and the like, should not be permitted to encroach upon the time devoted to the speakers, and those speakers themselves should be kept strictly within the bounds of the time designated. Treat all impartially. No matter if the most influential and honored speaker of the convention is addressing the audience, call him down promptly when his time is up, and if he is a true Christian he will thank you for it as heartily as his hearers. And even if the audience urge the continuance of the address, do not submit. The speaker that follows has rights that the audience is bound to respect. At the very opening of the session announce your purpose to hold to programme limits, and make this announcement so plain that all will understand it.

To Each a Part. — The more Endeavorers you can interest personally in the meetings of the local unions, the better will those meetings be. To this end a programme for the entire year, made out beforehand, is of great assistance. If copies are furnished the Endeavorers of the union, their thoughts will have something to fix upon. If they cannot attend one meeting, they will have it in mind to attend the next.

For the assigning of special parts in these meetings, the following blank may be found useful:

Dear Endeavor Friend: — The next meeting of our city Endeavor union will be held in the .... Church,

Sunday .... 3 P. M.   M .... will lead, with
the topic: .... Your part will be ....
Will you kindly accept the part assigned you, and assist in
making this meeting one of the best yet held?   Thanking
you in advance for your co-operation, and praying that
God may continue to bless our efforts " for Christ and the
church," we are

Yours in Christian Endeavor,
THE EXECUTIVE COMMITTEE.

Overflow Meetings. — If you can get all the Christian Endeavorers that are attending the convention
into one hall, even then I should advise the holding
of overflow meetings, in order that the citizens of
the place who in their homes are doing so much for
the convention, may have an opportunity to attend.
The Endeavorers may well be kept in one meeting
while the citizens attend the other, but the speakers
should be largely the same, and always the very best
convention speakers should go also to the second
meeting, if they are physically able to do so.

Sometimes the emergency is such as to compel the
getting up of overflow meetings on the spur of the
moment.   Usually, however, the need can be fore-
seen and provided against; and a good presiding
officer will always have in mind some plan that he
can carry out for the manning of an overflow meeting.

The speakers at these meetings should be as
evenly balanced as possible, and in order to provide
against a rush to one place and a second delay while
the overflow crowd is going to the other church pro-

vided, it is well, at the previous session, to divide the audience into two parts, requesting the Endeavorers in each portion of the audience to go to different places.

The Use of Dodgers. — If your hall will permit a large attendance from the locality, the best way to get it is by having printed notices, giving the whole programme, distributed from house to house. This calls the attention of the citizens to the meeting far better than a mere notice in the town paper, or a notice from the city pulpits, though these, of course, should also be given. If the weather is unpropitious, the use of these dodgers is especially important.

Lunches At Conventions. — It is a good plan, when a local union holds a convention of two sessions, to ask the delegates to bring lunches from their homes. Much pleasant sociability will be developed as these lunches are eaten, and the heavy tax on the local forces will be avoided.

Report the Conferences. — Whenever in your convention you hold simultaneous conferences, be sure that a bright practical report from each conference is given before the entire convention.

It is not usually best, though it is customary, for the chairman of these conferences to make the report. He is so busy in managing the conference that he is not able to take notes, and many of the practical and most pointed suggestions he fails to retain in memory. This is why the reports for these conferences are so often nothing but glittering generalities. Appoint a good speaker from each conference whose duty it be will be to watch the proceedings of the conference, take careful notes, and bring before the convention just the things that are brightest and most helpful.

A Model Meeting. — Occasionally, instead of the conferences for committee work, so common and so helpful features of our State conventions, it is a good plan to have before the entire company of Endeavorers a model business meeting, conducted upon the platform, with model reports from the chairmen of the different committees. In this way the entire audience gains a series of exceedingly practical suggestions regarding committee work, and possibly as much is received as could be gained from committee conferences.

A Bird's-Eye Meeting. — A pleasant plan for a union gathering is a meeting solely devoted to the presentation of Christian Endeavor work in all its many phases. One speaker will tell about Christian Endeavor work in Great Britain; another will give items about the societies that make up the United Society of Christian Endeavor of Japan; another will speak of the societies of China; others of the Australian societies, those of India, of Africa, of Europe, of South America, of Canada, and so on.

One of the Juniors may speak about Junior Christian Endeavor. The Floating Societies will not be forgotten, nor the societies in unusual places, such as prisons, in the army, in poorhouses, asylums, orphans' homes, and among the various foreign nationalities that have settled in the United States, such as Chinese, Greeks, Bulgarians, and Italians.

Attention should also be given to the different lines of committee work and the great endeavors of the society, such as those for Christian citizenship, systematic giving, missionary studies, Bible-reading, and the like. A word should be said about the great Conventions, and the history of the society in general. Such a meeting as this would serve not merely to inform outsiders of the scope and purpose of the society, but would undoubtedly interest, instruct, and stimulate the Endeavorers themselves.

Convention Bible Schools. — In some largely attended conventions, the delegates come in such crowds as almost to overwhelm the local Sunday schools. In such cases it may be well to hold convention Bible schools at several convenient centres, presided over by the best Bible scholars out of the many the convention will draw together. The names of these should not be announced beforehand, but the Endeavorers should be assured that they will get profit and pleasure if they attend the ones nearest to their boarding places.

Convention Evangelistic Meetings. — It is more and more becoming the custom to hold in connection with State and International conventions special evangelistic meetings, in factories, on the streets, on the wharves, in jails, and in all places where can be gathered a crowd that especially needs the gospel.

The usual time for holding these services is the noon hour. Careful preparation should be made beforehand by a committee whose sole work in connection with the convention should be these evangelistic meetings. Employers that at first refuse to give permission for the holding of these services are uniformly enthusiastic when they see the good results obtained.

One earnest Christian worker is to be placed in charge at each station where services are to be held. He will gather about him a group of fifteen or twenty earnest Endeavorers. The exercises at each place must be lively and yet deeply spiritual. Testimonies should be very brief. There should be much singing and much praying. Earnest prayers should precede the meeting. If the band can hold a few moments of prayer together before they go to the meeting-place, it will be the best plan.

There should be enough singing-books or leaflets for all that attend to have one. At every meeting appeals should be made for decisions for the Christian life. Reports from these meetings may be made by the workers at the sunrise prayer meetings of the following day.

Above all, after the more formal exercises of each meeting, the workers will talk face to face with the people they have come to help, seeking in these closing moments to gain positive results for the Master. Of course those that engage in such evangelistic undertakings should be careful to avoid anything like a patronizing way. Let them remember that many of those to whom they speak are, very likely, as genuine children of God as they themselves.

Denominational Rallies. — Denominational rallies on a large scale are possible only in connection with the International Conventions, and yet frequent experience has proved that it is possible to hold them at State conventions; and these small denominational rallies make up in the directness of their appeal to the individual what they lack in large numbers. They should by all means be held whenever the numbers attendant upon the State conventions will warrant.

The Closing Consecration Meeting. — Usually it is better for the address at the closing consecration meeting to be made by the man that conducts the consecration service. The meeting gains in this way a unity of impression that is quite marred by a new speaker.

Do not, however, place in charge of the consecration meeting one not familiar with this form of service. No one without a long training in Christian Endeavor conventions is likely to be competent to conduct this most spiritual of all meetings to the best possible advantage. The mistake most commonly made by those that conduct convention consecration meetings, when any mistake is made at all, is to talk too long themselves.

Convention Aftermath. — Sometimes it may be well to hold, on the morning following the closing consecration meeting of State conventions, an aftermath service, which is simply a sunrise prayer meeting held before the delegates take their trains for home. This service will be one of peculiar tender-

ness and beauty, and will gather up in many happy
ways the impressions and lessons of the convention.

Another kind of aftermath may be held, after the
fashion of some Massachusetts societies that had received a State convention into their midst. They
proposed to utilize the convention enthusiasm, and
for that purpose sent to all the members of the union
the following letter:

Second Baptist Y. P. S. C. E.

Dear Friend: We have had during the past week the
blessing of God with us in the State convention held in
our city, and the many things said and done during that
convention have inspired us all to do a greater work for
the Master. As soon as we are ready, God has promised
blessings.

Can we not, individually as well as collectively, make
the week of November 19 a week of prayer for guidance
as to the most profitable manner in which to carry forward
the banner of Christ?

Will you not, dear friend, go to God during the coming
week with the earnest prayer that he will endue us with a
spirit of consecration and love for his service and work?

Will you not, while the thoughts expressed at this convention are fresh in our minds, strive the more earnestly
to make the way of salvation so plain to others, that, with
the blessing of Christ, they may be made to see Christ as
he is and come out boldly in his service?

Yours in His name,

PRAYER–MEETING AND LOOKOUT
COMMITTEES.

Information Got Quickly. — Devote ten minutes of some session to asking each one present to name a place where, in his opinion, an Endeavor society might be formed, and also to name some person who might help start such a society. A few minutes of rapid talking and of note-taking will bring together information which months of correspondence would not gain.

Preliminary to the Open Parliament. — To make a successful open parliament the Endeavorers must be set to thinking beforehand along the lines of the topic to be considered. There is no better way to do this than by distributing, at the preceding session of the convention, slips of paper containing questions the delegates are expected to answer in the open parliament. Take for a sample the following questions for an open parliament on the work of the lookout committee.

Are You Interested in the Work of the Lookout Committee?

Note the following questions, study them, and be prepared with answers at the free parliament of the lookout committee, Wednesday afternoon.

"Come now, and let us reason together, saith the Lord." — Isa. 1 : 18.

1. — As a lookout committee, what is your plan of work at your regular church services?

2. — Is it a good plan to change the chairman *every* time officers are elected, especially if you have a chairman whose place would be hard to fill?

3. — What have you found to be the best method for handling the roll?

4. — How successful are you in getting members to send in "a message to be read in response to their names at roll-call, when obliged to be absent from the consecration meeting"?

5. — Do you look after the absentees from the first unexcused absent mark, or do you wait for the second or third?

6. — After a member has been absent from three consecutive consecration meetings, without a reasonable excuse, and having failed to win him back again, what is the next step?

7. — Have you any questions to ask or any plan of work to suggest that you have tried successfully in your own society?

8. — As a rule, the chairman of a committee does about all the work. As chairman of a lookout committee, have you anything different to report?

9. — How win associate members? Do you divide the associate list among the members of your committee, the same as the active? If so, for what purpose?

10. — Where does the work of the lookout committee end, that of the prayer-meeting committee begin?

11. — Have you successfully employed special methods to promote faithfulness to the pledge? Tell us about it.

12. — Do you believe in having a large affiliated list? If so, for what purpose, and how build it up?

13. — What does your lookout committee do for your Junior society?

14. — The revised pledge having been adopted by an executive committee of a society, but some of the mem-

bers opposing the change, how should the lookout committee work to overcome the objections, that all may be of one mind?

15. — What is the work of the lookout committee in the Sunday school?

" Therefore we ought to give the more earnest heed to the things which we have heard, lest at any time we should let them slip." — HEB. 2: 1.

A Written Open Parliament. — To carry on this exercise the best way is to print the programme with several blank pages, each headed by one of the questions to which answers are desired. If this is not done, blank pages headed in this way may be distributed at the beginning of the session in which the open parliament is to come.

Such questions as these may head the pages: How can we make the Junior meetings interesting? How can we get and keep the young men? What is the best feature of Christian Endeavor prayer meetings that you have tried? Five minutes may be given to the filling out of each of these pages, which will then be torn out and handed to the usher. The contents are to be read from the platform, and thus all that have good ideas to communicate will be able to present them, boiled down, and through the good strong voice of some one that will be able to make the whole roomful hear, and will enrich the suggestions with comments of his own.

CHAPTER XX.

THE PROGRAMME AND SPEAKERS.

Very Crowded Programmes. — Long observation of convention programmes has brought me to the conclusion that in no point are they so iikely to be in the wrong as in the matter of overcrowding. For some reason or other, probably because of the enthusiasm of the workers, no programme is so likely to be overcrowded as the programme of a Junior meeting, which of all others should be brief, on account of the tender age of the majority of the audience.

Not enough space is allowed in our programmes for announcements, singing, prayer, Bible-reading, the delays and hindrances that are almost certain to occur, and the possible though exceedingly rude over-stepping of their time by the speakers. It is always very easy to fill up the time if a programme is too short. Let the programme-makers err in this direction, and win the blessing of long suffering audiences.

The Printed Programme. — Let it be tasteful: a pretty programme is a neat introduction to the speakers. Let it be simple: an expensive programme cheats the mission-boxes. Let it bristle

with information concerning the principles and prac-
tices of Endeavor societies. Put it brightly, and not
catalogue-ly. The Endeavor pledge will leap from
the programme into many new hearts. Programme-
recognition of the officers and committees of the
union is no more than their due. The national mottoes and inspiring Bible quotations adorn a programme better than the printer's handsomest type.
If you have room, it is an excellent plan to insert the
words of the hymns to be used; and the best of
plans, to include helpful concert exercises and Bible
readings. Sometimes the programme may close with
the words of the Mizpah benediction. Find room,
if only an inch, for some account of the standing and
progress of the union, — a brief synopsis of the number of members of various classes, of conversions, of
money needed and on hand, of corresponding figures
for the last year or quarter.

The Speakers. — Never choose speakers merely
because of their reputation. Westfield's wire nails
may be the best of their kind, but they make poor
stuffing for a plum-pudding. Dr. Dryasdust may
have written a great commentary, but he is not,
merely on that account, a profitable speaker before a
convention of young people. Remember, too, that
a one-man convention is one half a convention. Regard fitness: the address of welcome to your most
warm-hearted man; the business meeting to your
most vigorous man; the open parliament to your
most suggestive man; the consecration service to
your most spiritual man. Do not select for speaker

the most brilliant writer and most charming man of the State, if his voice is inaudible at a distance of twelve feet. Bring in, if possible, one man from some other State or section of the State; fresh air comes in with him. The best method of obtaining speakers from the State is that in vogue in Connecticut, and to some extent elsewhere. A circular is sent out from headquarters to prominent Christian Endeavorers, asking for volunteer speakers, and a list of topics they would be willing to treat. It is well to send out a circular letter to prominent workers, asking for suggestions in regard to good topics and speakers.

The Topics. — Avoid general topics like " Christian Endeavor" and " Our Work " and " Duty." No matter how definite the treatment of such themes may prove to be, much of their value is lost because there has been no definite preparation for them in the minds of the hearers. Avoid sameness of topics. Scan carefully the late programmes of the union, and choose themes which have not been treated recently. Let a small part of the programme bear on outside causes, a still smaller part relate to topics of the day, and throw the main weight of the meeting in the direction of Christian Endeavor work proper. Do not shrink from emphasizing the leading Christian Endeavor features for fear the subjects are trite. Essential Christianity never becomes trite. The most essential matters, however, are made strangely inconsequential by a dull title; and bright statement of them will brighten the most commonplace subjects. In searching for fresh ways of putting things, however, the programme committee must fear the offence of mere " smartness " more than the fault of dullness. In the following pages the model meeting is resolved into its proper elements, and numerous topics are suggested under each head. Those in quotation marks have been used in conventions; those not so designated are, as far as we know, original with us.

Analyze the Topics. — Your audience will be likely to get more from an address if the principal points the speakers intend to make are briefly noted upon the programme. Sometimes it is best to divide the topic into several portions, assigning each portion to a separate speaker. There comes then the play of different minds, and the audience is less likely to become wearied.

The Address of Welcome. — Assign the address of welcome, if possible, to your best speaker. Nothing is so important as first things, and nothing is so hard to do well as commonplace things. The speaker may speak for the city government, for the church in which the convention is held, for the local Endeavor society or societies, or for the churches of the city. The response may be by the president of the union, by a visiting pastor or prominent worker. More than one address and response is almost certain to be tiresome; and even these, unless they are very " snappy." A printed concert exercise, with parts to be read alternately by hosts and guests, would make a pleasant variation. So would responsive verses of appropriate songs.

The Audience at Work.— Give the audience something to do every half-hour. Make them feel that they are running the convention; then all wheels will turn smoothly. Exercises for the drawing out and development of fresh talent are of double value; they take the convention from the domain of King Cut-and-dried, and they suggest speaking material for the next convention. The audience may be set to work in many ways. Let all heads bow in silent prayer at the opening. Call for sentence prayers, for concert repetition of the Lord's Prayer, for brief prayers on special topics. Make liberal use of responsive readings. Let your most able leader weave together by a few spiritual sentences a series of familiar songs on the same theme, to be sung by all, in spirited succession. Call out one-minute reports from societies, from district and county secretaries. Never omit the general question-box. A happy supplement is a question-box, at another session, on a single theme, as Junior work, inter-society visitation, the union lookout committee. A brisk variation, if you can find a sufficiently courageous man, is to set him forth to respond to oral questions from the floor. Another form of this most inspiriting part of the programme sets the leader to proposing problems, which are discussed by the members of the convention who are called out by the leader or by their own spirit. The results of these open parliaments should be presented compactly at their close, either by the leader, or, better, by some on-looker to whom the task has been assigned, and who has the grace of conciseness. Here are some themes for these general discussions : " Our Workshop, the Committees." " Our Legitimate Work, — what it is, and what it is not." " The Sword of the Spirit, and how to wield it." Senior Societies of Christian Endeavor, — what they are, and why they are needed. Dangers of the Christian Endeavor movement, and how tó avoid them. The Elements of the Model Christian Worker. How to Set People to Working. How has your Society Helped you? Which Element of Christian Endeavor work do you think most helpful? How can Religion be most attractively presented? The Exaltation of Christ in our Societies ; why and how?

Often it is well to hold simultaneous conferences on committee work and kindred themes. These should sometimes be formal, in part at any rate, and sometimes entirely conversation meetings. It is important, in all such cases of simultaneous meetings, to have five-minute reports of them before the entire convention, followed by an open discussion of these reports.

The Music. — Solo singing has its place ; but its place is never where congregational singing can well be introduced. It comes in well, however, in connection with congregational singing. Where the organ is a fine one, and the audience contains many country delegates, an organ recital will give great pleasure. A song service of fifteen minutes, especially a song service skilfully knit together by spiritual remarks from the leader, makes probably the best introduction to a session. Provide an abun-

dance of song-books.   Leave out preludes and in-
terludes.   Get a director who is spirited, but not
auctioneerish.   Let the president fill in the unex-
pected chinks with song.   Here are some topics for
song service: Sowing. The Parables. The Promises. Life and Death. Power and Weakness. Christ
in our Lives. The Bible. Work. Faith and Fru-
ition.   Our Master, Guide, Teacher, Friend and
Saviour.   Helping and being Helped.   Our Endeavors, What and Why.

The Consecration Meeting. — A consecration
meeting at the end need not prevent one at the
beginning. No topic of the programme needs such
careful selection as these.   They must be broad
enough to appeal to all minds, yet definite enough
to make a personal appeal to each mind.   Here are
some : " The Great Life-purpose."   " Soul-winning."
" Girded Thought and Service."   " Faithfulness to
Duty."   " Here am I, send me."   " Doing the Will
of Christ."   " The Secret of Power."   " Not Weary
in Well-doing."   The Sources and Power of a Holy
Life.   What Happiness is, whence it Comes, and
what it Accomplishes.   The Next Life : how to Prepare for it in this.   How to make Sin Fearful, and
how to take away the Fear of it.

The Presence of the Holy Spirit. — Prayer should
run, like a thread of light, through the whole of the
sessions.   Open with silent prayer, followed by brief
oral prayers of gratitude for the past, and petition
for the success of the convention.   Never omit that
rich fountain of blessing, the sunrise prayer meeting.

Draw the audience into all devotional exercises as far as possible. Let these exercises make up for their brevity by their frequency. If the sessions last over Sunday, always emphasize one fundamental Christian Endeavor principle by giving "Attendance on the local churches," a conspicuous place in the programme.

The Prayer Meeting. — It goes without saying that the central feature of Christian Endeavor work should be central in the discussions of Endeavor conventions. Especial pains should be taken to bring before the meetings accounts of fresh prayer-meeting ideas, and suggestive essays and talks by bright speakers. Introduce many topics like the following: "Why Separate Prayer Meetings for Young People?" "A Three-minute Paper on each of these: Preparing; Inviting; Attending; Leading; Singing; Testifying; Praying; Receiving; Rejoicing; Communicating." "The Responsibility of Leading a Meeting." "The Significance of the Consecration Meeting." "Witness-bearing." "Preparation for the Prayer Meeting." "How the Prayer Meetings may Lead to Conversions." "Christian Endeavor Graduates." "The Value of Expression." "The Prayers; the Praises; the Singing." "Hints to Leaders: Consistency of Life; What to Teach; How to Lead." "The Music: the Music Committee; the Chorister; the Organist; Selecting Pieces; Teaching Others to Read Music." "Prayer-meeting Ruts." "The Blessedness of Confessing Christ." "The Consecration Meeting an Incentive to Faithful Service." "How Far are We Individually Responsible for a Good Meeting?" "Suggestions for a Christian Endeavor Missionary Meeting, Temperance Meeting, etc." The Right and Wrong Use of Printed Comments on the Topics. How to get Thoughts. How to Gain Confidence in Public Prayer. Sanctified Ushers. Partnership with the Sexton. Music in the Meeting. How to Connect the Prayer Meeting with the Sunday-school Lesson Work. The Pastor in the Young People's Meeting; what he should do, and what he should not do.

For the Associate Members. — Endeavor societies are fed from below, from the Juniors; and from the side, from the Associates. Every convention should reach a hand down and a hand out, as well as stretch beseeching hands upward. Get conferences, symposia, or single papers on some such themes as these: "How can we Reach and Help our Associate Members?" "Our Duty to the Associate Members." "Two Open Letters: from the Active Member to the Associate; from the Associate Member to the Active." How to Freeze Out the Associate Members. Utilizing the Associates. When is it a Grace to be an Associate Member, and when a Disgrace? Getting Associate Members to Work for Each Other. The Advantages of Frank Talk with the Associates: who should do it, and how it is to be done? Things which Keep Associate Members from becoming Active Members. How to be an Active Associate Member. How to Associate with Associate Members.

The Juniors. — Work with the little children is
so recent among Endeavorers, is comparatively so
difficult, and is of such extreme importance, that
for some time every Endeavor convention, even of
but a single session, should bring out and inspire
some thought on the matter. Here are some hints
for subjects: "Two Views: (1) The Church With
a Junior Society; (2) The Church Without One."
"The Model Junior Meeting." What a Junior
Meeting is not. Talking Down to Children. How
to Attract Interest and Keep it. The Art of Illustration. The Use of Story-telling in Junior Work.
Dangers in Junior Work, and how to Avoid them.
Qualifications for a Good Worker among the Juniors.
How to get the Juniors to Co-operate with the Older
Endeavorers. How to Teach Little Folks to Pray.
Work in which Juniors most quickly Grow.

The Social Side. — Social endeavors always receive countless kindly illustrations in these conventions; but the theory of the social art may well be
discussed also. The papers here suggested may well
be followed by actual socials in the church parlors,
to practise their precepts. Select for these subjects
Endeavorers who will give large measure of practical direction and small measure of generalization.
"The Principal Object of Christian Endeavor Socials." "What Constitutes a Good Time?" "Do
our Socials Afford Opportunities to Win Souls?
How?" "How shall we Induce those not Christians to Attend our Socials?" "How Soon may we
Expect Right Results?" What Games should not

be Played at Christian Endeavor Socials? How
Christian Endeavorers may Entertain a Crowd. Play
and Profit. How to Lead and be Led in Socials.
How to Win the Associate Members through Socials.
Unsanctified Long Faces. All Society and no Christian Endeavor : how came it, and what's to be
done?

Other Christian Endeavor Features. — (*a*) THE
PLEDGE. "Keeping the Pledge in the Spirit or the
the Letter — which?" "The Cast-iron Pledge."
"The Pledge as a Stimulus to Christian Activity."
"The Three Elements of the Pledge: (1) Private
Devotion; (2) Support of Church Services; (3)
Public Confession." How the Pledge Becomes a
Burden; how it Becomes a Staff. Pledges Every-
where. Why Pledge-taking is Manly. Backsliding
from the Pledge : its Causes ; its Cures. Side-track-
ing the Pledge. Objections to the Pledge and their
Answers. Corollaries of the Pledge. Hidden Ele-
ments of the Pledge. How to Make and Keep the
Conscience Sensitive.

(*b*) THE COMMITTEES. "How to Develop Efficient Committees." "Faithfulness to Committee
Work." "Neglected Committees." "Calling and
Relief Committees : What and Why?" How to make
the Work of the Flower Committee Doubly Beautiful. Do we need New Committees? Have we too
many Committees? How to get Chairmen to Lead
and Committeemen to be Led. What is the Executive Committee to Execute? On what Committees
should none but Active Members Serve, and Why?

Humility and Vigor in Committee Work. What is the Usher Committee, and what may it Accomplish? By what Methods may the Good-Literature Committee gain Subscriptions for Church Papers? How and why should Old Papers and Magazines be Collected? Wherein does the Lookout Committee need to look out for itself? How may the Society help the Lookout Committee? The Value of Printer's Ink in Committee Work; the Danger of it. How to Revolutionize Reports.

(c) THE OFFICERS. "What are the Duties of the Corresponding Secretary?" How to gain Dignity, Promptness and Efficiency as a Presiding Officer. The Value of Records. What may a Treasurer do, besides Hold the Money? What Use can the Endeavor Society make of the Newspaper, and which Officer should do this Work? The Vices of Vice-Presidents. How not to Preside. Coquetting with one's Office. When is Office-holding a Duty? Preparing one's Successors. Office-holding and Office-filling. Magnifying one's Office: how and why.

(a) LOCAL UNIONS. CONVENTIONS. "Reports from Larger Conventions." "The Duties and Results of the Union Lookout Committee." "How can our Local Union Work be Improved?" "The Work of the District Superintendent, and how it may be made more Efficient." "How the Local Union may reach Churches having no Young People's Societies." "The Inter-Visitation Scheme." "What should I bring to the Convention, and what carry away?" Elements of Disintegration in Local

Unions: how can we neutralize them? One-man Power in Local Unions, and its Dangers. How to Perpetuate the Convention. The Unconventional Convention, and how to get it. What makes a Good Audience ?

(*e*) MISCELLANEOUS. "Enthusiasm in Christian Endeavor Work." "Why so Few Ideal Societies ?" "The Unifying Influence of the Y. P. S. C. E." "Why the Church should Welcome the Christian Endeavor Movement." "Evolution in Christian Endeavor." "Our Work: Duties to be Done; Dangers to be Encountered; Encouragements to be Given; Results to be Aimed at." "Our Central Idea." "The Line of Enlargements." "How to Develop the Latent Talent in our Societies." "The Young Christian's Duty to his own Church." "How can our Societies best reach Young Men ? — Young Women ? " "Permanent Elements of Christian Endeavor Societies." "The Society's Appeal to the Military Virtues." "The Society for Christ; for the Church; for Humanity." "The Daily Conduct of Christian Endeavorers." "What is your Aim, Endeavorer ? " "Danger Signals." "Some Conditions of Successful Endeavor Work." "Our Watchwords: Duty (to the Church); Loyalty (to Christ); Fellowship (one with another)." "The Mary and Martha Sides of Christian Endeavor Work." "The Field for Christian Endeavor Work." "How can Christian Endeavor Societies be carried on Successfully in Small Towns ? " "Nineteenth Century Societies." "The Necessity for Prayer in our Meetings." "Is the Y. P. S. C. E. a success?"

" Soul-winning the Ultimate End of Christian Endeavor." " The Society as a Circulating Medium for
Religious Reading." " The Badge we Wear, and
why we Wear it." " Christian Endeavor Fellowship."

Kindred Causes. — We are proud of Christian
Endeavor, but that pride must not blind us to the
other noble movements of the religious world.
Every convention is the better for shaking hands
cordially with one or more of these.   A few of such
kindred causes are here mentioned: " The Ideal
Sunday."   " The Sunday that we can Realize."
" What can Christian Endeavor do to secure better
Sunday observance ? "   " The claims of the Ministry
on Young Men."   Christian Endeavor for the W. C.
T. U. and the Y.'s.   The various organizations for
systematic Bible study, and how can we use them in
our Societies ?   How the Y. M. C. A.'s and Y. P.
S. C. E.'s occupy entirely different Fields.   The
White Cross Work.   Christian Endeavor for the
Indian.   The Country Week, and our Stock in it.
Good Government, and how it Depends upon the
Minors.   The Unique Features of the Christian
Endeavor movement, and Reasons for Insistence
on the Christian Endeavor Name.

The Conduct of Life. — Our pledge is so inclusive
that any ethical question is properly discussed before
a convention ; for have we not promised to do as our
Master wills in all things ?   Organizations are alive
only as they bear fruit in lives.   And so one such
topic as the following may well appear on every

Christian Endeavor convention programme: " Fidelity." " The Secret of a Happy Life." " Take a Higher Plane." " Sanctified Endeavor." " Satisfactory Service." " What of it ? " " The Christian's Influence upon his Every-day Associates." For a series: " The Young Christian can help his Church by ————; his Pastor by————; his Brother by ———." " World-wide Movements for Christ." " Power for Service." " The Christian in the World." " The Maximum Christian." " Christian Growth." " Christian Steadfastness." False Recreations.

The Bible. —Christian Endeavorers delight in the Bible, and so should their conventions. Above all things, do not assign the Bible-reading of the meetings to a man whose voice is feeble and articulation muddled, and who reads without spirit and understanding. If any exercise deserves impressive delivery, this does. Nor is it the easiest thing in the world to prepare a Bible-reading and make it effective before an audience; rather is the task one of the most difficult in the world, requiring not only ingenuity and spirituality, but the best of literary and oratorical art. Honor the Bible in these ways, in concert and responsive readings, and in frequent papers and discussions like the following: " The need of a Bible Training-Class in each Society." " The Sword of the Spirit." " How to Read the Bible in Private Devotion." " Bible Study essential to Spiritual Growth." " Methods of Bible Study Preparatory to Personal Work." " How to Preserve the Proper Balance of Scripture, Testimony and Prayer." "How to Study the Bible." "How to Use the Bible to Win Souls." "The Method of Bible Study best suited to our Societies." "God's Word in Christian Endeavor Work." The Misuse of the Bible. The Helpfulness of Concordances and Bible Indexes. The Use and Abuse of Commentaries. How to Mark a Bible. How to Study the Bible with others. Daily Readings : at what Hour? how Long? in what Manner? Private Reading for Public Use. How to become able to Quote the Bible well.

Missions. — Get news from headquarters, if you can : find a real live missionary to talk to you. Deal sparingly in letters from abroad ; letters, especially from busy people, are usually unsatisfactory, except to personal friends. Remember that Endeavor is Christian and can expect the prosperity of Christ only as, with Christ, it goes into all the world. Give large room to such themes as the following : " Missions : our Duty towards them." " In Darkest New York." " Personal Missionary Work." " Systematic Christian Endeavor in Evangelistic Work (1) In the City; (2) In the Country; (3) Around the World." " Why should I be a Foreign Missionary?" " Why should I support a Foreign Missionary?" " The Joy of Giving." Polyglot Christian Endeavor. How to Support a Missionary. Systematic Giving : what it is, and what it does. The Two-cents-a-week Plan. Offertory Calendars. **Missions in the Home. Neighborhood Missions.**

Missions in Odd Places. Missionary Triumphs. For abundant additional topics see Mr. Mershon's excellent pamphlet, " Portfolio of Programmes for Missionary Meetings," and Miss Brain's " Fuel for Missionary Fires," both published by the United Society.

Temperance. — Prominent among the allied causes in which all Endeavorers take an interest is the temperance movement, and every convention programme should give wise direction to this interest.   Let such topics as these be discussed : What Constitutes Intemperance?   Intoxicants which are not Alcoholic : their Use and Danger.   Alcohol in Disguise.   What does it Cost?   Christ's Life a Temperance Sermon. Drunkards who are not Drunk.   What are some of the False Remedies for Intemperance?   What is the only Foundation for a Temperate Life, and why ? Organized Temperance Efforts, their Power and their Need.   How can Children be helped toward Temperance, and help others ?   Good Plans for a Temperance Prayer Meeting.   Temperance Endeavors in small towns ; in cities.

Looking Backward and Forward. — Insert just enough about the past to make a good stepping-stone toward the future.   Christian Endeavor is to make history, not to gloat over it.   Conventions must gather up results ; but their chief work is to inspire to larger results.   The model programme will contain one feature looking (though the metaphor is a comical one) both backward and forward. These topics will suggest others : " A Decade of

Progress, a Decade of Promise." "Larger Results
— how Conditioned." "The State Convention of
189– : what the Convention expects of us ; what we
expect of the Convention." " Shall there be an Advance Movement in 189– ? (1) The Spiritual side
of our work made pre-eminent. (2) More aggressive
Personal work for Christ." " The Backward and
Forward look of the Society: Backward, to the
Juniors ; Forward, to the Church." " A Symposium.
What can we put into our work, the coming year, to
to make it more efficient ? (1) More Consecration.
(2) More Enthusiasm. (3) A stronger Allegiance to
the Pledge. (4) Faithfulness to Committee Work.
(5) Loyalty to our own Church. (6) Making our
Religion more Practical. (7) Quality, not Quantity." " Some things New and some things to Re-
new in Christian Endeavor work." " What for the
Future : Winter Quarters, or a Campaign ? "

For Pastors. — Every Christian Endeavor convention should emphasize the fact that Endeavorers
honor their pastors, and seek in every way to be
subordinate and helpful to them. Room should
always be made for a convention sermon, even if it
be only a ten-minute sermon. Introduce pastors'
half-hours, in which the pastors, by representatives
of the several denominations included in the union,
or in a manner more free, may give and receive
Endeavor inspiration. By pastors and by laymen
let such topics as these be discussed : " How has
the Y. P. S. C. E. benefited my Church ? " " The
Endeavorer in the Sunday evening Service: (1) As

the Pastor views it; (2) As the Members view it."
" How may the Society help its Pastor ? " " How
may the Pastor help his Society ? " " The Ideal
Pastor for a Christian Endeavor Society." " The
Ideal Attitude of the Church toward the Society."
What relation should exist between the Officers of
the Church and of the Society ? Societies which
Push the Church, and Societies which are Pushed by
the Church. How to crowd the Mid-week Prayer
Meeting. What Endeavorers want in the Sermon;
What the Sermon wants in Endeavorers. The Pas-
tors who do not Attend their young people's meet-
ings. The Crusade against Pastors' Opposition:
What the Young may do; What other Pastors may
do.

Business. — Usually the only collection taken
should be to supply the absolutely necessary funds
for carrying on the union. Union meetings should
not be used as conveniences to raise money for local
causes, or for schemes which any well-meaning phi-
lanthropist may bring to your attention. The be-
nevolence of Endeavorers should go through their
own churches to their own denominational causes.
This is the universal rule. Great attention should
be given to this point. Do not let your union, State
or local, be used as a money-raising convenience.

All the grace of the prayers and the papers may
be neutralized by a graceless business meeting. Let
the business meeting be an anticipatory illustration
of the consecration meeting. Open it with prayer,
conduct it with prayer, and close it with prayer.

A good outline for the meeting is the following:
"Minutes. President's Report. Secretary's Report.
Treasurer's Report. Report of the Union Lookout
Committee. Report of the Extension Committee.
Report of the Nominating Committee. Election of
Officers. Miscellaneous Business." The reports of
the various officers and committees of the Union
should be briefest of the brief, boiled down to the
point of interest. These topics may excite helpful
discussions of such matters: " Business Methods
in Christian Endeavor Societies." " Money in the
Lord's Work." " The Model Society Business Meeting." (Five-minute reports from different committees.) How may the Business Meeting be made a
Training in Christianity ? What are the Dangers
of the Business Meeting ? What Society Business
may be Transacted on Sunday, and under what Circumstances only? What are the Causes of Unbusi-
ness-like Methods? Good Ways of Raising Money.
Wrong Ways of Raising Money. Organization a
good Servant but a bad Master. How to gain
Business-like Habits, and how to help others gain
them. How it Helps a Society to take up a Collection in it. To what Objects may a Christian Endeavor Society be asked to Contribute Money?
Stationary *vs.* Perambulating Contribution-boxes.
What may Executive Committees Accomplish for
the Good of the Society?

Closely Woven Meetings. — For the sake of unity
and of novelty it is a good idea sometimes to plan
for an entire convention whose sessions shall be knit

together by some central idea of manifold out-reachings. The following schemes will suffice to illustrate: "*Lessons from Saint Paul for Christian Endeavorers:* (1) Advice Concerning the Character which Active Members Should Maintain; (2) His Example Respecting Questionable Acts or Employments; (3) His Ideas Concerning Prayer meetings; (4) Paul as a Member of a Lookout Committee: (5) Paul on the Missionary Committee; (6) Paul's Method of Reaching Associate Members; (7) Paul's Enthusiastic Loyalty to Christ; (8) Paul's Consecration to Service." *The Little Giant, Christian Endeavor:* (1) Its Eyes, the Lookout Committee; (2) Its Mouth, the Prayer-meeting Committee; (3) Its Ears, the Music Committee; (4) Its Hands, the Social Committee and the Executive Committee; (5) Its Feet, the Missionary Committee; (6) Its Brain, the Good-Literature Committee; (7) Its Backbone, the Pledge. The Vertebræ of the Backbone. (8) Its Heart, Christ. *The Lord's Prayer Convention:* (1) Our Father: the Christian Endeavorer's Leader; (2) Hallowed be thy Name: the Art of Prayer; (3) Thy Kingdom: the Weakness and Strength of Modern Missions; (4) Thy Will: Consecration an Active, not a Passive, Condition; (5) Our Daily Bread: Things to be Thankful for; (6) Our Trespasses: the Struggle Between Sin and Endeavor; (7) Our Temptations: the Dangers in the Way of Christian Endeavor; (8) Thine the Glory: the Final Triumph of Christian Endeavor, —when and how? In similar fashion may be worked out: The Beatitudes Convention, The Parable Convention, The Convention of Promises, The Convention of Prophecy, and so on.

The Arrangement of the Programme. — In arranging the programme, two rather opposing ends are to be sought: the meetings must have symmetry and continuity, and yet monotony must be avoided. Watch with especial care the question of time. Cut your coat according to your cloth, and do not expect to get a two-days' programme out of ten hours. Leave interstices throughout the programme, into which papers and discussions may stretch if they must; only, keep this provision a secret from the speakers!

The Temple Series

4 3-4 x 7 1-4 inches. Dainty cloth bindings. Illustrated.
Price, 35 cents each, postpaid.

This is the handsomest series of holiday books at a low price ever issued. The books are by the best modern authors They are beautifully bound in cloth of dainty shades, stamped with an original cover design in colors and gold. Each volume contains an appropriate half-tone frontispiece.

The Four G's...........................By Theodore L. Cuyler.
Grace, Grit, Gratitude and Growth.

Golden Counsels...........................By Dwight L. Moody.
Practical subjects forcefully presented.

Well-built...................By Rev. Theodore L. Cuyler, D.D.
Plain talks to young people.

Helps Upward.....................By Rev. Wayland Hoyt, D.D.
Apt illustrations of great themes.

A Fence of Trust...........................By Mary F. Butts.
Poems and Sonnets.

Pluck and Purpose...................By William M. Thayer.
Success, and how to attain it.

Little Sermons for One......................By Amos R. Wells.
Heart to heart talks.

Wise Living.................By Rev. George C. Lorimer, D.D.
The gaining and wise use of money.

The Indwelling God.......By Rev. Charles A. Dickinson, D.D.
The power and purpose of a life of faith.

Tact...By Kate Sanborn.
Racy essays on society's virtues and foibles.

Youth and Age....................By Rev. James Stalker, D.D.
A suggestive treatment of Ecclesiastes 12.

Sunshine (Poems)...........................By Mary D. Brine.
Poems of cheer and encouragement.

Making the Most of Oneself......By Rev. A. S. Gumbart, D.D.
Practical talks to young men.

Answered! By Rev. J. Wilbur Chapman, D.D., Rev. R. A. Torrey, D.D., Rev. C. H. Yatman, Rev. Edgar E. Davidson, Thomas E. Murphy, and Rev. A. C. Dixon, D.D.
Remarkable instances of answered prayer.

Just to Help...................................By Amos R. Wells.
Some poems for every day.

Old Lanterns..........................By Rev. F. E. Clark, D.D.
Valuable lessons from Jeremiah.

UNITED SOCIETY OF CHRISTIAN ENDEAVOR
Boston and Chicago

The Deeper Life Series.

A series of daintily bound books upon spiritual themes by the leading religious writers of the age. Bound in uniform cloth binding. 6 3-4 by 4 1-2 inches in size. Price, 35 cents each.

The Inner Life. By Bishop John H. Vincent, D. D.

"A study in Christian experience" which shows how the life of the soul is the true reality, and what striking results are wrought when the power of Christ and the indwelling of the Holy Spirit become the controlling forces in a life.

The Loom of Life. By Rev. F. N. Peloubet, D. D.

"The threads our hands in blindness spin,
Our self-determined plan weaves in."

"The Loom of Life," and "If Christ were a Guest in our Home," which is also included in this volume, are two very helpful sketches by the author of that well-known publication, Peloubet's "Select Notes." Many new and forceful truths are presented, such as will give the reader thought for serious consideration for many a day. The book abounds in apt illustrations and anecdotes, in the use of which Dr. Peloubet is so skilful.

The Improvement of Perfection.
By Rev. William E. Barton, D. D.

This is not a treatise on the higher life, but is meant to help young Christians to a higher life by showing what kind of perfection God expects, and how it is to be gained, at the same time furnishing an incentive to attain it. The aim is practical rather than theoretical, and the style is clear and attractive.

I Promise. By Rev. F. B. Meyer.

The book is appropriately called "I promise." Its chapters deal with matters of the utmost importance to every Christian, such themes as "Salvation and Trust," "Winning God's Attention," and "What Would Jesus Do?" In strong, sensible, winsome words the path of duty is pointed out, and conscience is spurred to follow it.

UNITED SOCIETY OF CHRISTIAN ENDEAVOR,
Boston and Chicago.

The "How" Series.

By AMOS R. WELLS.

7 1-4 by 4 1-2 inches in size. Uniformly bound in cloth with illuminated cover design. About 150 pages each. Price, 75 cents each.

How To Work.

This is a working nation, and yet few among its millions of workers know how to work to the best advantage and with the best results. The fundamental principles of wise labor are set forth in these chapters in a familiar, conversational style. Much of the book consists of actual talks given to young men and women starting out in life. "Puttering," "Putting Off," "Hurry Up!" "Taking Hints," "A Pride in Your Work," "'Can' Conquers," "The Bulldog Grip," "The Trivial Round,"—these are specimen titles of the thirty-one chapters. The book is not didactic, but presents truth in illustrations, so that it *sticks*.

How To Play.

The author of this book evidently believes in recreation. The very first chapter is entitled, "The Duty of Playing." Separate chapters are devoted to the principal indoor amusements, conversation and reading being the author's preferences, and also to the leading outdoor sports, especially the bicycle and lawn tennis. There are many practical chapters on such themes as how to keep games fresh, inventing games, what true recreation is, and how to use it to the best advantage. "Flabby Playing," "Playing by Proxy," "Fun that Fits," "Overdoing It,"—these are some of the chapter titles. In one section of the book scores of indoor games are described, concisely, but with sufficient fulness.

How To Study.

These chapters, on a very practical theme, deal with the most practical aspects of it,—such topics as concentration of mind, night study, cramming, memory-training, care of the body, note-taking, and examinations. The author makes full use of his experience as a teacher in the public schools and as a college professor, and the book is largely made up of talks actually given to his students, and found useful in their work. The chapters are enlivened by many illustrations and anecdotes, and the whole is put into very attractive covers.

UNITED SOCIETY OF CHRISTIAN ENDEAVOR,

Boston and Chicago.

Recent Religious Books

The Secret of a Happy Day
By Rev. J. WILBUR CHAPMAN, D.D.

6 3-4 x 4 1-2 inches ; 103 pages ; bound in cloth. An excellent half-tone portrait of Dr. Chapman forms the frontispiece.
Price, 50 cents.

The " Daily Quiet Hours " at the Detroit Christian Endeavor Convention were the most remarkable meetings of that great gathering. The addresses given by Dr. Chapman at that time have now been divided into thirty-one chapters, — one for each day of the month — and are included in this volume. The first edition of the book was sold out upon the day of publication. A new edition is now ready. The chapters of the book are based upon the wonderful twenty-third psalm.

The Spiritual Life of the Sunday-School
By Rev. J. WILBUR CHAPMAN, D.D.

6 -34 x 4 1-2 inches, 62 pages ; bound in cloth, 35 cents.

These articles were originally printed in the *Sunday-School Times*. There was such a demand for them that Dr. Chapman has now consented to put them into this permanent form. The book presents very clearly the duties and opportunities of both officers and teachers, and gives some suggestive helps on the preparation necessary for personal work.

The Surrendered Life
By Rev. J. WILBUR CHAPMAN, D.D.

6 3-4 x 4 1-2 inches ; 70 pages ; bound in cloth ; 50 cents.

This little volume sets forth clearly, simply, and winningly the life "hid with Christ in God," and the way to enter into it. The tasteful binding forms a most fit setting for the contents.

UNITED SOCIETY OF CHRISTIAN ENDEAVOR
Boston and Chicago

www.ingramcontent.com/pod-product-compliance
Lightning Source LLC
Chambersburg PA
CBHW020041040426
42331CB00030B/120